RUSH HOUR

Talk Radio, Politics, and the Rise of Rush Limbaugh

RUSH HOUR

Talk Radio, Politics, and the Rise of Rush Limbaugh

by Philip Seib

THE SUMMIT GROUP ~ FORT WORTH, TEXAS

⌣

The Summit Group

1227 West Magnolia, Suite 500, Fort Worth, Texas, 76104

Cover Photograph by Peter Liepke
Page Design by Troy B. Reese
Cover Design by Sean Walker
(ISBN: 1-56530-100-5)

For Christine

Contents

PREFACE

For anyone interested in the political mood of America, listening to Rush Limbaugh's radio show is essential.

Make no mistake, the views Limbaugh and most of his callers express are not universally held. This is conservative politics—Ronald Reagan territory. Government is too big, social programs are a waste, abortion is a sin, news media are too liberal...the litany is extensive.

Limbaugh's radio program showcases the frustration and anger that characterize so many Americans' attitudes about politics. This dissatisfaction is not limited to conservatives; the feeling extends across the ideological spectrum. It becomes manifest in calls to talk shows, in votes for Ross Perot, and in a belief that America—as nation and ideal—has gone astray.

Many of Limbaugh's callers are exceptionally articulate advocates for conservative positions on issues ranging from health care to foreign aid. Limbaugh is equally articulate as their cheerleader. He insists to his fellow conservatives that, despite the results of the 1992 presidential election, "We are winning."

His premise is that Bill Clinton and the Democrats are digging a deep hole in which they soon will be trapped. Escalating taxes and heavy-handed governance, says Limbaugh, will precipitate a conservative rebellion.

That is speculative, but far from speculative is Limbaugh's enormous appeal and success. The chapters that follow offer recitations of his ratings points, book sales, newsletter subscriptions, and other measures of his growing one-man media empire. Awash in the millions that his enterprise has generated, Limbaugh is bemused by detractors who cannot figure out how a secular preacher of politics can attract and hold such a following.

A big part of the answer has nothing to do with politics. Limbaugh is a superb entertainer. He understands the difference between talking *to* and talking *with* an audience; he recognizes the value of persistent self-promotion; he knows how to leaven serious issues with humor. Even liberals who can't abide his politics may find themselves chuckling if they tune in his radio or TV show.

Rush Hour is not a biography. More interesting than Limbaugh himself is the Limbaugh phenomenon—his ability to mix politics and entertainment, and attract audiences numbering in the tens of millions.

In politics, Limbaugh is Ronald Reagan's ideological descendant, a leader of the conservative opposition to the Clinton administration and the Democratic Congress. After the unsatisfactory Bush interregnum, many on the Republican Right look to Limbaugh as champion of a purist revival. They cheer him as he bashes liberals and other ne'er do wells.

Limbaugh's style owes as much to entertainers as to politicians. His approach is an amalgam of the techniques of Huey Long, Will Rogers, Arthur Godfrey, and many others who have used the airwaves successfully.

His success is also attributable to the rising popularity of talk shows. This is yet another indicator of public frustration with traditional political institutions. With diminished faith in electoral politics, people look for alternative ways to express their needs and wants, hopes and fears. Talk shows are an appealing venue.

Because of its increasing importance, talk radio itself is worth examining—its history, the techniques of those who preside over its programs, and the potential dangers if it is used thoughtlessly or maliciously.

After Election Day 1992, many in the broadcast industry speculated that Limbaugh would fade back into obscurity. Without a partisan battle dominating the daily news, a combative polemicist would presumably become irrelevant.

Far from fading away, Limbaugh's star began to shine even more brightly after the election. People did not put their political interests into storage; they wanted to keep talking about them. Limbaugh encouraged them and gave them a forum...and they responded. By all statistical measures, his success continues to increase steadily.

Given his apparent staying power, Rush Limbaugh—the man, and the political and entertainment phenomenon—deserves scrutiny. *Rush Hour* looks at how he got here and where he's going.

ACKNOWLEDGMENTS

Thanks are due to a number of people who helped create this book:

- Vanessa Polak, my research assistant, worked swiftly, thoroughly, and cheerfully, always meeting whatever absurd deadline I set for her.

- Mike Towle and Mark Hulme, my editor and publisher at The Summit Group, were steadily supportive. When decisions had to be made, they made them wisely and promptly.

- Christine Wicker, whom I already knew to be the best spouse anyone could hope for, also was patient advisor and thoughtful editor. Without her loving support, this book could not have been written.

DITTOHEADS ON THE MARCH

"Greetings conversationalists across the fruited plain! Saying more in five seconds than most talk show hosts say in an entire show...with talent on loan from God...holder of the prestigious Attila the Hun Chair of the Limbaugh Institute for Advanced Conservative Studies...doing this show with half my brain tied behind my back to make it even...I will again refute those who demand equal time, because I am equal time!"

Watch out environmentalist wackos, feminazis, animal rights extremists, multi-culturalists, and trendy lefties. Rush Limbaugh is on the air.

In his own words, he is, "A man, a legend, a way of life." Three hours a day, five days a week, carried by more than 625 radio stations, reaching roughly twenty million listeners each week. Add thirty minutes daily for a TV show with steadily climbing ratings. Those numbers and that daily exposure just begin to define the Rush Limbaugh phenomenon.

Republican leader William Bennett is one of Limbaugh's political mentors. He is effusive about Limbaugh's importance. Limbaugh, he says, "may be the most consequential person in political life at the moment. He is changing the terms of debate. He is doing to the culture what Ronald Reagan did to the political movement. He tells his audience that what you believe inside you can talk about in the marketplace. People were afraid of censure by gay activists, feminists, environmentalists—now they are not because Rush takes them on. And he does it with humor. We have a reputation as somewhat prim and priggish, and Rush is absolute death to liberals: a conservative with humor."[1]

MEDIA CLOUT

In 1988, Limbaugh was merely another local talk show host, enjoying life in Sacramento, California, a mid-size media market far removed from the pressures of national attention.

Within five years—by the time Bill Clinton moved into the White House—Limbaugh had become the leading voice of conservatism.

His clout made him the envy of politicians. With a few well-chosen words, he could enrage yet another million liberals or precipitate enough telephone calls to overwhelm the U.S. Capitol's switchboard.

Along with political clout, he established a personal empire that encompasses the radio show, the syndicated television program (carried by more than two hundred stations reaching 97 percent of the country as of mid-1993), one-man "concert" appearances, best-selling books, a newsletter (with close to four hundred thousand subscribers), T-shirts, fan clubs, and just about anything else that might win a follower or make a buck.

Here's one example of how the Limbaugh machine generates dollars. He plugs his newsletter on his show and provides an 800 phone number for ordering. Call it and a briskly efficient operator offers you one year for $29.95 or a two-year bargain for $49.95. The operator takes your credit card number at high speed and disconnects quickly, moving on to the next caller.

Call another number and you can order from the Limbaugh merchandise catalog. How about a nice "Rush" coffee mug, or a bumper sticker proclaiming, "Rush Is Right"?

One disconsolate Limbaugh fan told his hero that his wife wouldn't let him spend their money on the newsletter. Limbaugh gave constant on-air plugs to the bake sale the fan was holding in Fort Collins, Colorado, to raise the thirty bucks. To put it mildly, the leader's word helped. Approximately thirty-five thousand people showed up, and Limbaugh himself jetted in.[2]

He even has his own lexicon. For example, many of his followers refer to themselves as "dittoheads." This derives from Limbaugh's effort to stop his worshipful callers from spending air time praising him. After all, he knows they all love him. So, he told them just to say, "Ditto," and the message would be delivered. This led to callers conveying "Megadittos from Tampa" and the like, and so to the birth of "Dittoheads."

Picking up the nuances of this vernacular requires listening to the program several times (as Limbaugh himself admits), but soon the lingo begins to make sense. It's one of the ways Limbaugh bonds with his fans in a massive private club.

PRESIDENTIAL POLITICS

Limbaugh and his principal medium—talk radio— came into their own during the tumultuous 1992 presidential race. For many who thought they understood American politics, this was the year of the world turned upside down. Here were the Democrats finally running a competent campaign. Here was George Bush—Gulf War and opinion poll champion—in free fall. And here was a fast-talking, faster-spending billionaire tapping into a huge reservoir of voter dissatisfaction.

Politicians and the reporters who covered them were fascinated by topics most people couldn't care less about. "Issues" such as adultery and draft-dodging made headlines, while millions of Americans either were losing their jobs or fearing they soon would.

As the insiders played "gotcha" and touted the horse race, the public—shut out and ignored—fumed. Of the politicians, Ross Perot seemed to have the best sense of what was happening, but his idiosyncrasies limited his appeal.

Lack of an acceptable candidate was frustrating, but not so much so that people were willing to abandon politics.

The issues of the moment were sometimes important, sometimes not. This variety was not unusual. More than a hundred years before, Alexis de Tocqueville had observed, "All the domestic controversies of the Americans at first appear to a stranger to be incomprehensible or puerile, and he is at a loss whether to pity a people who take such arrant trifles in good earnest, or to envy that happiness which enables a community to discuss them."

Regardless of the weight of the issues, opinions were still passionately held. If only there were a way to express them. If only someone who shared their irritation would give them a chance to be heard.

For millions, the knight riding to the rescue was Limbaugh. Armed with fluent conservative rhetoric and waspish humor, Limbaugh rallied and empowered the faithful. He preached and his listeners—using their telephones—did so too. If Clinton, Bush, and Perot wouldn't talk straight, Rush and his audience would have their own dialogue.

For Rush Limbaugh, 1992 was the perfect time for professional ascendancy. He met a perceived need, saying what many people wanted to hear.

He might not have attracted much notice at some other times. In 1984, for example,

Limbaugh probably would have seemed an irrelevant echo while Ronald Reagan convinced voters that his conservative revolution was producing "morning again in America." That year, satisfaction with the status quo helped Reagan carry forty-nine states. Outrage—at least among most conservatives—was unnecessary.

Eight years later, conservatives felt betrayed by George Bush. He had abandoned his "no new taxes" pledge and offered only unconvincing endorsements of right to life and other litmus-test positions. As much as they were disenchanted with Bush, conservatives saw Bill Clinton as a terrible alternative. Here was a smart, tough liberal—no pushover like George McGovern, Walter Mondale, or Michael Dukakis. Clinton had a Reagan-like intuitive understanding of the electorate, and knew how to enshroud Democratic liberalism in a smoke screen of centrism. After winning five of the past six presidential elections, conservatives realized their White House tenancy was now imperiled.

They were not alone in their anguish. Uneasiness transcended ideology. The situation was like that in the transitional 1980 election, about which political scientist John Kenneth White observed, "A values gap between the governed and the governors had become one of the dominant features of American life."

Problems were daunting. The vast national deficit—understood by few, worried about by many—made true economic recovery unlikely. Congress was plagued by scandal, lobbyists, and gridlock. Other nations—especially Japan—threatened America's economic dominance. The end of the Cold War created more uncertainties than it resolved. The only consistency in the news was the stream of layoffs.

The sour mood was reflected in two best-selling books: Ross Perot's *United We Stand*, in which the first chapter is titled "An America in Danger," and *America: What Went Wrong?*, by Pulitzer Prize-winning reporters Donald Barlett and James Steele.

While Perot tried to build a base broad enough to produce an electoral victory, Limbaugh had no need to venture beyond his own ideological turf. His popularity was partly due to public anger about the state of politics, but his constituency was almost exclusively conservative. In his broadcasts, personal appearances, and his first book, *The Way Things Ought to Be*, Limbaugh embraces the tenets of Republican conservatism.

By no means is he an extremist or a polarizer such as David Duke. Limbaugh's positions are conservative, but most are conventionally so. His pronouncements, although often bombastic, are usually free of bitterness. One of his greatest assets is a touch of self-mocking humor that he injects into what otherwise could become a tedious tirade. For instance, when he claims to be "documented almost always right 97.9 percent of the time," he disarms at least some of those angered by his positions.

A FAITHFUL AUDIENCE

As intriguing as Limbaugh himself is, so too are the media (principally radio) and politics that have made him so influential. His power comes from his audiences. His relationship with them says something about the continuing evolution of American democracy.

This is not a matter for the select few. Political change is constant; the process responds—even if sluggishly—to people and issues, and it adapts to the exigencies of the moment. During Limbaugh's rise, one of the most significant political changes was the real or threatened unemployment of many white collar workers, men and women unaccustomed to being so badly battered by the economy.

Although Limbaugh's detractors might characterize his audience as being mostly bigoted, semiliterate yahoos, substantial numbers of his listeners are those worried white collar workers. These are Republicans and Democrats who voted for Reagan twice and Bush once, but came into

1992 scared and looking for alternatives. Some stuck with Bush, some drifted to Clinton or Perot, but many were searching for a place besides the ballot box where they could register their dissatisfaction. Listening to and calling Rush Limbaugh was one of their few options.

Also among Limbaugh's fans are conservative college students. They, too, are unhappy with the available crop of politicians. So while they await a candidate for whom they can muster some enthusiasm, they treat Limbaugh like a rock star.

Certainly, he has his share of droolers, too, but attempting to wrap the Limbaugh audience into a nice, neat stereotype is unwise.

Limbaugh's critics also claim that he appeals to the worst instincts of his listeners, nourishing their prejudices. On the other hand, a case can be made that Limbaugh is really a democrat (very definitely with a small "d"). For those who call in to his radio program, he provides an alternative to silent frustration. For those who hear or read his policy pronouncements, he provides stimuli that counteract apathy. They listen, they think, they agree or disagree, they call—they participate. Bringing this about is an important contribution and should not be dismissed out of hand.

Understanding Limbaugh's clout requires understanding the subtleties as well as the dramatic events of politics: the post-Reagan conservative drift; the long-in-coming pragmatism of moderate liberals; the vacuum created when false conservatives and false liberals dominate their parties. These are among the factors producing an audience that wanted and needed a Rush Limbaugh.

We live in what has often been proclaimed to be "the age of television." Certainly, the rise of television's pervasiveness, popularity, and power during the past half-century is remarkable. But TV is not the sole medium on which people depend. Many read, even if not as often or as much as they once did. And many listen to the radio.

With commuting times lengthening for many people, the radio is a more constant companion. A 1991 survey found that the average American spent three hours each day listening to the radio, compared to four hours and nine minutes watching television.

Although Limbaugh is something of a one-man multimedia conglomerate, radio remains his principal link to his public. He is part of a long tradition of radio masters—politicians such as Franklin Roosevelt and Huey Long, and entertainers such as Arthur Godfrey and Jack Benny.

Within the world of radio, the talk show is increasingly popular. According to *Broadcasting* magazine, 875 radio stations used "talk" to describe their format in 1992, up from 238 stations just five years before. Surges like that don't happen just because some radio executives decide they like talk shows. Ratings, not whims, drive programming. People are listening to talk radio in growing numbers. These programs are interactive bulletin boards for local communities and the nation. People are interested by them and depend on them.

Their audiences also like them partly because they provide a counterpoint to standard news programming. These shows allow listeners to be active participants, not merely passive recipients.

You can't talk back to Tom, Peter, Dan, and Connie, or the other sages who tell you each evening what you're supposed to be thinking about. Television rarely even offers any vehicle comparable to print media's "letters to the editor" columns. The talk show, however, lets its listeners call in to comment and advise and argue…to take over from the all-knowing anchorperson, even if just for a few moments.

As cable television's capabilities expand, perhaps it will cut into talk radio's popularity. The national town hall sessions that Ross Perot advocated might let people feel they have more control over political events. But until that happens, Limbaugh and his talk show colleagues are likely to see their influence grow.

BLAST AWAY

Rush Limbaugh's clout certainly isn't due just to format. He is an ideologue and makes the most of it. His litany is that of the Reagan conservative, with none of the restraint a vote-conscious elected official finds necessary. When examining his pronouncements, you can find a factual error here, an arguable interpretation there, and an aggravating absolutism almost everywhere.

But Limbaugh doesn't care. Ready, fire, aim. He blasts away and hits his targets often enough. If a few shots go astray, so what?

Even though his philosophizing might not measure up to academic standards, his message must be taken seriously; the numbers require it. For example, consider his book, *The Way Things Ought to Be*. By September 1993, when it completed a full year on the *New York Times* best-seller list, close to three million people had bought the $22 volume. The hardcover version remained a best seller even when the paperback was published and immediately became the number one softcover best seller. That means something; you don't sell that many books if people think you're a fool.

Most of the twenty-seven short chapters address issues framed by Limbaugh's mix of anecdote and argument. At the root of many of his positions is his affinity for the 1980s—the Reagan years. Denounced by some as an era of greed and corruption, this decade is defended by Limbaugh as the heyday of entrepreneurship and national resolve.

That interpretation of history will retain its appeal if the economy remains sour and the Clinton administration falls on its face. If, however, Clinton accomplishes much of what he has promised, Limbaugh's premise might come to seem archaic. He can keep pounding away at Clinton, but he will need a base broader than Reaganism on which to stand. Limbaugh or someone else will have to define a conservatism for the 1990s and make a case for it.

But for now, Limbaugh's legions are devoted, as *Washington Post* columnist William Raspberry found out. Limbaugh had praised something the liberal Raspberry had written. Raspberry decided he could do without Limbaugh as a fan and said so in a column, clearly implying that he considered Limbaugh a bigot.

Raspberry then heard from some sixty zillion readers (his estimate) who said, basically, "Prove it." The columnist—who admitted he hadn't known much about Limbaugh when he criticized him—found he couldn't. He didn't like what Limbaugh had to say about many issues, but he admitted this didn't make Limbaugh a bigot.

So, Raspberry apologized. Score one for the dittoheads.

Another facet of Limbaugh's appeal is his use of different forums. His base remains the radio show, but his TV program is increasing in popularity. Its executive producer is Roger Ailes, mastermind behind such television triumphs as "The Mike Douglas Show" and George Bush's 1988 campaign advertising. It lacks some of the radio format's verve because it has no call-ins. But it attracts sponsors and a hard-core audience. Ailes says of Limbaugh's TV skills, "Rush has brains, a sense of humor and he's the best improvisational performer since early Jack Paar."[3]

Limbaugh also has what he calls his "concerts"—personal appearances to preach his political gospel on college campuses and elsewhere. He keeps his true devotees happy with the subscription newsletter, and he undoubtedly will find additional ways to get the Limbaugh message to a still larger public. Like Michael Jordan in commercials, Limbaugh is inescapable.

Also like Michael Jordan, Limbaugh is the centerpiece of a personalized conglomerate. His varied enterprises—all derived from the radio show—are making him very rich. Estimates of his 1993 earnings range as high as $15 million. His diversified ventures are likely to make his public life-span longer than that of many media "personalities."

His commercial success ensures that imitators will appear, but few are likely to feature the combination of self-confidence, intelligence, wit, and performer's zeal that makes Limbaugh such a formidable presence.

CONSERVATIVES' ALLY

The future of the Rush Limbaugh phenomenon is about more than Rush Limbaugh. It depends on and will affect the course of politics and the role of the mass media.

For conservative politicians, Limbaugh will continue to be a useful ally, keeping the faithful enthusiastic and serving as a warm-up act for the next band of Republican would-be presidents. For liberals, he will remain a nuisance, denigrated by those who differ with him but grudgingly respected because of the size of his following.

At least as interesting as Limbaugh's own prospects are those of his fans. With as many as twenty million people estimated to be listening to Limbaugh during any given week, his audience constitutes a potentially significant chunk of the electorate. (The higher-than-usual turnout in the 1992 presidential election was 101 million voters.)

Politicians surely contemplate what these people might do during the next several years. Will they be content to stick with Limbaugh, letting their anger ebb and flow with his rhetoric? Will they become so exasperated with politics that even Limbaugh is unable to hold their interest? Or, might they form a legion of support for a particular candidate, similar to the Perot volunteers of 1992?

Of course, the likely answer to each of these questions is, "That depends." No evidence exists that the Limbaugh audience is monolithic. Also, answers would vary according to the state of the political environment. If, for instance, the economy takes a significant turn for the better or for the worse, the size and mood of Limbaugh's audience presumably would shift accordingly.

But given the incremental pace of most political change, plus Limbaugh's shrewdness and his fans' devotion, his influence is likely to remain fairly constant during the foreseeable future.

Talk radio will continue to be an important forum for political expression, and Limbaugh will remain, as he puts it, "on the cutting edge of societal evolution." He is a force to be reckoned with.

JUST A HARMLESS LITTLE FUZZBALL

Who is this guy?

The basic biography reveals nothing special. Rush Hudson Limbaugh III—known at home as Rusty—was born in 1951 in Cape Girardeau, Missouri. He grew up in a stolidly Republican household: both parents were active in the GOP; a grandfather was Dwight Eisenhower's ambassador to India; an uncle is a federal judge appointed by Ronald Reagan.

Early on, he became fascinated by radio, and did imaginary play-by-play sports broadcasts. In high school, he was a member of the football and debating teams, but they couldn't hold his interest. In today's terms, he was a nerd. He rarely went out on dates and never owned a pair of blue jeans.[1]

By age sixteen, he was working for a local radio station, moving up from general helper to disc jockey. He modeled himself after Chicago D.J. Larry Lujack—"the only person I ever copied," says Limbaugh.[2] After one unhappy year in college (at hometown Southeast Missouri State), he dropped out to begin the nomadic life of a broadcaster. He used names such as Rusty Sharpe and Jeff Christie, read the news, was a D.J., and did talk shows.

Some foreshadowings of the later Limbaugh appeared. For instance, in 1974 he greeted listeners of Pittsburgh's KQV with, "Good evening to you, music lovers, across the fruited plain."[3] By the 1990s, that had become, "Greetings, conversationalists, across the fruited plain."

He also got fired several times. And, while working in Kansas City, he got married...twice. Neither marriage lasted.

Giving up on radio at one point, he went to work for the Kansas City Royals baseball club, handling group ticket sales and special events. He says, "The only time my politics got me in trouble was when I engaged Hal McRae and Amos Otis in a debate about the players' union."[4] He still counts Royals great George Brett as one of his best friends.

After five years with the Royals, he tried radio again. As a newscaster for Kansas City's KMBZ, he riled management by adding his opinions to news reports. For example, he illustrated the "new ideas" of presidential candidate Gary Hart by offering thirty seconds of silence.[5]

His controversial style and corporate infighting at KMBZ led to yet another firing. In late 1984, Limbaugh moved on to KFBK in Sacramento, which liked their talk shows lively. Limbaugh followed the recently fired Morton Downey, Jr., who had been sacked after making what was perceived as an ethnic slur on the air.

In Sacramento, Limbaugh was a hit—"a huge whale in a sauna," as he puts it. He convinced his bosses that he could make a talk show work with no guests, and he mastered the art of being interesting without being bizarre and offensive, as Downey had seemed to many to be. Describing his approach to an interviewer, he said, "I want controversy because of the issues, not because of rudeness or abruptness with a caller." He nearly tripled his audience in a year and kept refining his style.

As a celebrity and Sacramento's top radio star, he was riding high. Then he began thinking about ways to go national.

Enter Ed McLaughlin, former president of ABC's radio network and an independent producer and syndicator of programs such as Dr. Dean Edell's medical advice show. He had heard about Limbaugh, so he went to Sacramento to sample the work of this prospective client. Sitting in his hotel room, he listened to Limbaugh on the air and was unimpressed. He thought, "He sounds like a real braggart." But he met with Limbaugh and then listened to him on the air again, this time while driving around in a car, as many of Limbaugh's listeners did. His opinion changed: "If you're driving and things are distracting, it's easy to tune out. I found myself not tuning out with Rush."[6]

McLaughlin and Limbaugh entered into a high-risk partnership. They wanted a daytime, national talk show, and they wanted to call the shots about format and content.

They cut a deal with WABC in New York. Limbaugh would get the noon until two slot for a national show available to ABC network stations that wanted it. WABC provided studio, engineers, telephones, and staff, all for no charge. In return, Limbaugh had to do a WABC local show from ten until noon, also for free. These local hours, says Limbaugh, constituted the capital he was investing in the venture.

Limbaugh began his local show on July 4, 1988, and the national program on August 1. He started with fifty-six stations and a total daily audience of 250,000, most of whom were listening just to the local WABC show. (The New York station did not carry the national program at first.)

He was up and running. Within three months, the show was being carried by more than one hundred stations. And, not surprisingly, controversy was sprouting. A South Bend, Indiana station, after a spate of complaining calls from viewers, notified Limbaugh that it was dropping his show. Limbaugh countered. He went on the air with this message: "Ladies and gentlemen of South Bend. A concerted effort to censor this show has begun. As we speak, a few angry liberals, precious guarantors of the First Amendment that they claim to be, are calling the station demanding that this show be taken off the air....If you love this show—and you know you do—you must let the station know." The tactic worked; the South Bend station was deluged with calls not only from local listeners, but also from Limbaugh fans around the nation. The show remained on the air in South Bend.

While dealing with occasional problems like that one, Limbaugh kept building his audience. He went on the road almost every weekend, appearing before groups in cities where his show was heard.

He took another big step toward national prominence with a November 1990 appearance on "Nightline." Here he was not a political entertainer, but rather a serious, forceful advocate of the U.S. military build-up in the Persian Gulf. Debating the issue with liberal commentator Mark Shields, he defined his position tersely: "We're going to turn back aggression and we are going to maintain the free flow of oil at market prices. And I think those two objectives are noble and valid, and I think the American people support them." Further, he defended his radio audience, rebutting Ted Koppel's suggestion that Limbaugh's listeners who supported intervention were under informed.[7]

The "Nightline" invitation was not extended to Limbaugh just so he could offer his own opinions. After all, he had never pretended to possess special expertise about the Middle East. Rather, he was there as the spokesman for his constituency—the audience that was so devoted to him. Rush Limbaugh as acknowledged representative of the masses (or at least the conservative masses); that was a role he was to assume more and more often.

Limbaugh flavors his political pronouncements with a brashness that has its own humor. Similarly, he defines his show's success with egocentric braggadocio. For example: "The primary purpose of callers on my show is to make *me* look good, not to allow a forum for the public to make speeches." Some people might find that boorish, but it makes sense. As Limbaugh says: "Two minutes of a boring caller is the same as playing a song nobody likes. What do you do when a song you don't like is played? You go looking for a song you do like."[8]

Behind all this bluster lurks a gentler soul. In the course of a lengthy interview with Limbaugh, *New York Times* reporter Maureen Dowd found that "his off-the-air personality is far less brazenly assured." He seems to be a shy workaholic: "I'm going to stay hot as long as I want to stay hot, and that's directly relatable to how much passion I have about my work. I love what I do. It's other stuff that bores me. I don't live for weekends. I have a vacation coming up...and I haven't the slightest idea what I'm going to do. There's nowhere I want to go." He adds, "I like to veg" on weekends.

He also is something of a sentimentalist. Asked about his favorite movie, he told Dowd: "I loved the ending of *Love Story*. I'm an incurable romantic."

After two divorces, his romanticism is tinged with caution. He admits to dating liberals and to contemplating having a family, and he's not above talking wistfully to an interviewer about being in love.

Don't feel too sorry for him. With his newly acquired millions, he can indulge in some far-from-ordinary pastimes. For instance: "I sometimes charter a jet and go somewhere for dinner"...somewhere such as New Orleans or San Francisco.[9]

This hardly seems to be the portrait of a cunning manipulator of political opinion. Limbaugh often characterizes himself as "just a harmless little fuzzball." Perhaps. But don't try to sell that description to someone whose favorite cause or beliefs have just been run over by the Limbaugh steamroller.

RUSH ROOMS

At lunchtime in the River Bank Restaurant and Lounge in Mishawaka, Indiana, the conversation is hushed. The chewing of hamburgers and slurping of soup is accompanied by a sonorous voice piped in for a few hours each weekday. Some of the diners nod in agreement, some just listen. That Rush Limbaugh sure knows what he's talking about.

This is the River Bank's "Rush Room." Limbaugh's staff estimates there are more than three hundred such gathering places around the country. A restaurant or bar can proclaim itself a Rush Room, or, if it buys advertising on the local radio station that carries Limbaugh, it will be designated an "official" Rush Room.[10]

The owner of the River Bank estimates his business is up substantially since he opened the Rush Room. He even shows tapes of the previous night's Limbaugh television program each evening on a large-screen TV in the restaurant. He and local Dittoheads like the Limbaugh-oriented community they have established.

The River Bank's Rush Room opened in 1988 and its popularity has endured. In the autumn of 1993, the restaurant reported that its Rush Room business "keeps growing and growing."

This is an intriguing measure of the dedication of Limbaugh's followers. Presumably there aren't three hundred Jay Leno or David Letterman Rooms around the country, and it's doubtful that many restaurants serving Sunday brunch feature David Brinkley or "Meet the Press" Rooms.

Limbaugh calls his show "the only healthful addiction in America." Apparently he does have his addicts.

GROWING NUMBERS

The Limbaugh legions continue to grow. His radio program enjoys the largest audience of any radio talk show since the advent of television.[11]

In the cutthroat competition for advertisers, radio stations wield Limbaugh's ratings aggressively. For example, WBAP Radio in Fort Worth, Texas, sells time with this message: "During 'The Rush Limbaugh Show,' WBAP is the No. 1-rated station with adults eighteen and over. Rush Limbaugh is the most listened-to radio program, day or night, in North Texas."

Further, Limbaugh has given a boost to AM—as opposed to FM—radio. In Dallas-Fort Worth, for example, not only is WBAP the highest-rated station during the Limbaugh show, but also it is the only AM station in the top ten at that time.

An analysis of Arbitron radio surveys by Limbaugh's syndication company, EFM Media, shows a steady climb. Average quarter-hour-listenership (the Arbitron measure) has risen from about 250,000 in November 1988, to 3.83 million in February 1993. In six of the nation's fifty biggest media markets, Limbaugh's show is the top-rated program on any station and at any time of day. From February 1992 to February 1993, Limbaugh's audience increased 58 percent.[12]

This is an interesting figure, because a post-election dip might have been expected. But with such an inviting target as the young and stumbling Clinton presidency, Limbaugh has had no trouble fashioning audience-appealing commentary.

The Dittoheads have some consistent characteristics. According to a July 1993 *U.S. News and World Report* survey, Limbaugh's audience is 96 percent white, 58 percent male, and 55 percent Republican.

The core constituency is adults twenty-five to fifty-four, two-thirds of whom are men. Baby boomers and Limbaugh are on the same wavelength. According to talk show analyst Michael Harrison, these listeners "perceive news and current events as pop culture," viewing the Persian Gulf War, for example, as a "CNN miniseries."[13] For them, Limbaugh's mix of entertainment and serious issues is appealing.

JUDGING NUMBERS

Journalists, politicians, and entertainment professionals have mixed opinions about Limbaugh.

Ted Koppel says: "He clearly has become something of an icon to millions of conservative listeners. He's very smart, he does his homework. And you ignore him at your peril."[14]

According to ABC's Jeff Greenfield: "His reach is to a new segment of conservatives: working class, younger, humorous. They love satire, they like rock 'n' roll music. And Rush Limbaugh, among other things, is really funny."[15]

Mary Matalin, Republican-campaign-strategist-turned-talk-show-moderator, says: "He is a new animal, which is why people have a hard time defining him. They want him to be fish or fowl, an entertainer or an ideologue, but he is none of the above."[16]

Actor Harry Shearer, who hosts his own politico-comic radio show, is not impressed by those who attack Limbaugh's virulent conservatism: "This country runs on personality, not ideas. I think if Rush were spouting diametrically opposed ideas, he'd be just as popular. The only people he is dangerous for are the people in time slots opposite him."[17]

Similarly, Norman Lear, television producer and founder of the liberal People for the American Way, says: "Real passion is at such a premium these days. In the land of the sitting and reading dead, Limbaugh's got passion, and thus he's watchable."[18]

Critics, however, abound. Larry King, whose claim to political talk show dominance has been usurped by Limbaugh, says, "I don't think he's funny."[19]

Sharper words come from Senator Tom Harkin (Democrat-Iowa): "We always have people like this. They feed on fears and appeal to the darker side of human nature. But they don't last long—people catch on to them."[20]

Alexander Cockburn, columnist for *The Nation*, says: "Humor always helps. But he seems to me the last surviving idiocy of the Reagan-Bush years. It's like those stars that give off light long after they've died. Long after everything Reagan-Bush stood for has collapsed into disaster, the sound waves continue, and you hear this mush peddler carrying on."[21]

And columnist Erma Bombeck dismisses him as "Rush Slimebaugh."[22]

Multiply these comments by a few million. Just about everyone who has heard Limbaugh has an opinion about him. The July 1993 *U.S. News* survey found Limbaugh to be less popular than Oprah Winfrey and Phil Donahue but better-liked than Pat Robertson and Jesse Jackson. Among his listeners, 47 percent agreed with most of his issues positions, while 23 percent disagreed.

The audience size and the conviction underlying both praise and criticism of Limbaugh are striking, particularly because of the suddenness of his rise. The Rush Limbaugh empire certainly has taken hold and is growing. Reasons for this exist beyond the ideological and entertainment-related dynamics of the Limbaugh juggernaut.

POLITICAL ANGER

One of the most highly praised non-fiction books of the early 1990s is *Why Americans Hate Politics*, by E.J. Dionne, Jr., a reporter for the *Washington Post*. The book is about the failure of both liberalism and conservatism, the triumph of symbols over substance, and other flaws in America's political life. As important as the book's contents are, the title by itself reflects the mood of much of the nation.

But this "hatred" of politics does not necessarily overwhelm interest. People might hate the way Washington works, but still realize they have a big stake in the outcome of those workings. These mixed feelings are evident in the comments of callers to Limbaugh's show.

Another aptly titled book is *Mad As Hell*, a chronicle of the 1992 presidential campaign by columnists Jack Germond and Jules Witcover. This title, too, says much about the public's attitude toward politics.

It is derived from Paddy Chayefsky's film *Network*, in which a deranged anchorman urges his viewers to vent their anger: "I want all of you to get up out of your chairs. I want you to get up right now and go to the window, open it, and stick your head out, and yell, 'I'm as mad as hell and I'm not going to take this any more!' "

Of course, as the authors note, Americans did not decide merely to scream about the sad state of affairs; instead, "they trooped to the polls on Election Day...and voted in record numbers and in percentages not attained since John F. Kennedy narrowly defeated Richard Nixon" in 1960.[23]

The anger the authors of these books perceived is not the product of an innate mean-spiritedness. Mainstream American politics certainly can become nasty; some campaigns feature as much mud as was produced by the Midwest floods of 1993. But most Americans want their system to work; they hope their country and their fellow citizens—including their elected officials—will do well.

While not malevolent, many Americans are frustrated. A 1991 study conducted for the Kettering Foundation found that Americans were not apathetic about politics, but believed that they could have no impact and that politicians did not understand their problems.

A general disquietude had settled around issues such as the national debt and imbalanced trade. Few people understood the economic principles involved or saw how these matters were directly affecting their household budgets, but they still knew that something was wrong. They sensed that the system needed fixing, and probably with a major overhaul rather than a mere tune-up.

The frustration was exacerbated in 1992 by what Republican pollster Bob Teeter called "a unique recession." Although blue collar workers had learned that layoffs are just an unpleasant fact of life in their jobs, they expected to be put back to work after a few months. That wasn't happening during this recession. According to Teeter, in most bad recessions, only about 15 percent of workers permanently lose their jobs. In the "Bush recession," the figure was closer to 40 percent. Also, middle-income white-collar workers—who weren't used to being laid off—were suddenly facing unemployment.[24]

Although the number of unemployed men and women hovered around ten million, several times that number were worried about job security. In addition to dooming George Bush's reelection effort, this anxiety produced a desire to go beyond traditional politics and the ballot box. People wanted—needed—to vent frustration and seek solutions to the country's apparently insoluble problems.

Limbaugh's role in such situations can be viewed in two ways. Either he provides a useful outlet to help relieve systemic stress, or he makes things worse by stoking resentment and reducing issues to unrealistically simplistic terms.

His critics insist the latter is true. For instance, Brian Keliher of San Diego, publisher of the anti-Limbaugh *Flush Rush Quarterly*, says Limbaugh will not face up to the complexity of the issues he addresses. He also criticizes what he says is dittoheads' robot-like adherence to the Limbaugh canon.

Keliher monitors Limbaugh's shows and writings, and challenges questionable facts and opinions. His newsletter provides ammunition for those who want to argue with dittoheads.

If he is guilty of oversimplifying, Limbaugh certainly is not alone. One of the byproducts of high-speed information delivery—whether by television, radio, computer network, or other mechanism—is a shrinking of collective patience. If Tom, Dan, Peter, Bernie, or any other newscast anchor—or Rush—can explain a problem in a minute, it can't be too complex. So, why can't it be resolved? For example, if a week's worth of fighting in Somalia can be crammed into a two-minute TV news package, how much trouble could it possibly be to negotiate peace?

Such expectations are rooted in the prompt resolution of conflict on television sitcoms. If Bill Cosby could cleverly and humorously resolve this week's domestic crisis, why should any household have problems? Despite Oprah's and Phil's focus on the dysfunctional, nothing seems unreasonable about smoothing life's road—making the complex simple and the laborious easy.

Those who govern find that this way of thinking makes their jobs more difficult. Sometimes referred to as the "fast-forward effect," this acceleration of expectation is rarely compatible with the realities of designing and implementing policy. So if Rush Limbaugh or anyone else says,

"The federal deficit can be wiped out in three years," those who must actually make it happen—and who know that at least ten years (or whatever) will be needed to do the job—are aghast. They realize that they, not the glib prognosticators, will have to take the heat from the impatient public.

Limbaugh is far more sophisticated than are most commentators who make a living by generously dispensing their wisdom. Nevertheless, he is a major contributor to the fast-forward effect as it alters public perception of many issues. Public impatience fuels his popularity, so he has a vested interest in nurturing that impatience.

As Limbaugh's popularity rose, he certainly was aware of the concurrent rise of public anger about the state of politics, specifically about what he called "the failure of the grand liberal social experiment." Citing this as the cause of the upsurge in hostility toward politicians, he said: "The American people are blamed for homelessness; they're blamed for AIDS; when they get tax cuts, they're blamed for causing the deficit. They're tired of taking all this blame for problems they didn't cause."[25]

Regardless of whether all the blame should have been dumped on "liberals," the public was fed up. Limbaugh's audiences grew, and so did support for another master of the clever phrase, Ross Perot.

A MAVERICK HERO?

Perhaps Perot will end up a historical footnote—an electoral oddity like Robert LaFollette and George Wallace. Or maybe he'll someday talk and spend his way into the White House.

Whatever the future might hold, he certainly made his point in 1992, winning more than nineteen million votes—19 percent of the total cast. Restructuring the campaign agenda through the force of his personality, he made Bush and Clinton talk about the deficit, an issue they presumably would have preferred to pretend didn't exist.

As maverick hero, he gave millions of disaffected Americans an alternative to "none of the above" as their choice for president. He tapped the discontent by presenting himself as an outsider who could challenge the Washington establishment. At the same time, he portrayed himself as an embodiment of American ideals.

In doing so, Perot followed the course set not just by fellow 1992 candidates Paul Tsongas and Jerry Brown, but also that of the ultimate insider-outsider of recent years, Ronald Reagan. Hardly an outsider when he was the incumbent president, Reagan nevertheless managed, "to the frustration of his political opponents, to present himself as the righteous outsider to the government he led. More than just an outsider, Reagan stood, like the citizen heroes of American myth, as the redeemer of American individualism and idealism."[26]

In 1992, the mood was right for a reincarnation of the outsider hero. Voters weren't merely wistful about better political days, they were furious about the current state of affairs. In focus groups conducted by the Bush campaign in April, people who had supported Bush in 1988, but were now undecided, were "angrier than the Republicans had ever imagined. Bush neither cared nor understood the concerns of ordinary Americans," they told the focus group coordinator. "And when pushed to pick between Bush and Perot, they picked the unknown Perot overwhelmingly, a man about whom they had learned nearly everything from magazine shows, talk shows, features and word of mouth—and almost nothing from the establishment press."[27]

Perot and anger went well together. In their post-election analysis of the campaign, journalists Jack Germond and Jules Witcover wrote, "Perot sought to mobilize all the apprehension, frustration, fear and anger in the country through the force of his own rather quirky personality and immense wealth, and fashion it into an effective political tool."

Along the same lines, CBS pollster Dottie Lynch said of Perot: "He was rage. He was alienation."[28] And that made him news.

Exchanges between Rush Limbaugh and his listeners also reflect rage and alienation. Like Perot, Limbaugh served as a lightning rod for outrage. Limbaugh, however, is in many ways more credible than Perot. As a vote-seeker, Perot's motives were bound to be questioned. That is simply part of politics. Also, although news coverage of him was erratic at best, Perot found himsel frequently on the defensive. Fighting with reporters and putting out brush fires set by Bush or Clinton partisans preoccupied Perot. Such distractions pulled him away from delivering his message.

Limbaugh didn't have to endure that. He could hammer away, day after day. He wasn't asking anybody for votes, so his motivation was not at issue. The increasing press attention he was receiving was far gentler than that which any candidate could expect.

Despite these differences, Limbaugh and Perot also had much in common. For instance, among Perot's earliest supporters was a group called THRO—Throw the Hypocritical Rascals

Out. Its members were non-politicians fed up with politics as usual—the kind of people who nodded in agreement and pounded their fists on the kitchen table when they heard Limbaugh blasting Congress's latest folly. These were the "owners" to whom Perot wanted to return the country.

Limbaugh knew the Perot people were out there. He told an interviewer: "I talk to Perot people on my show, and meet them when traveling around the country. They are upwardly mobile, middle- and upper-middle-class people, who are just fed up with what they see as the decline of the country. They may not be able to voice it, it may be in their subconscious, and Perot is bringing it out."[29]

In June 1992, Limbaugh offered a thoughtful appraisal of Perot's popularity. "I think Perot convinces people that they matter again, that they're relevant, that what they want is what should happen. His message is, 'You own the country and we won't do anything until you say we should do it.'

"Say what you want about his lack of

specificity, he's also the one candidate who doesn't run from a problem...He makes people think that, by virtue of his presence, things are going to happen that haven't happened. It's his presence, the fact he's on the scene. The specificity of 'how' is irrelevant to them at this point."[30]

But Limbaugh came to mix his praise of Perot with tough criticism. In *The Way Things Ought To Be*, Limbaugh says of Perot: "His is one of the best psychological appeals in years....Millions of Americans rejoice because someone in the political world is finally standing up for them and thanking them for the contributions to the greatness they have made, rather than accusing them of being the reason for the nation's decline." But, says Limbaugh, Perot's candidacy was not created by spontaneous public demands that he run. "Believe me, Ross Perot leaves nothing to chance. It is not his nature. This is pure deceit..."[31]

In July 1992, when Perot dropped out of the race, Limbaugh said the Texan "had a performer's ego," and that his rationale about not wanting the election to end up deadlocked and thrown into the House of Representatives was merely "the most convenient reason he can find to avoid blaming (his withdrawal) on himself."[32]

Tension between Limbaugh and Perot is virtually inevitable as a function of jealousy about claiming the title of "Number One Outsider." Limbaugh is likely to prevail because he is more consistent about his issues and apparently is not prone to the odd personal behavior that has damaged Perot's credibility.

Both men are probably happy to keep out of each other's way. Each has plenty of his own business to attend to.

What remains interesting is that their ascendances were concurrent. This says something about public perceptions of political America: realization that the country is off track, insistence on blunt talk from those who shape public opinion and public policy; and general impatience with the status quo.

DISTRUST OF THE MEDIA

This public anger about politics is accompanied by growing distrust of the news media. Limbaugh says: "The media is now considered just another part of the arrogant, condescending, elite, and out-of-touch political structure...engaging in the abuse of power." He contends that the news media's problems fall into the general categories of accountability, responsibility, and attitude. As is the case with many of his issues positions, he won't find much argument about that from most of the country.

By no means is Limbaugh the media's only harsh critic. For example, the watchdog organization Accuracy In Media (AIM) purchased a large advertisement in the September 27, 1992, *New York Times* that was headlined, "A Message to the TV Networks from Your Viewers: We're Fed up with Negative, One-Sided, Distorted TV News!" It included the following passages: "We're a group of Americans who are sick and tired of how you in Television News, especially the famous network anchors, are using slanted, biased, deceptive news in a blatant attempt to manipulate public opinion....We're mad at the way you're trying to influence the election by making sure you always find something critical or negative to say about candidates you want to lose, and show candidates you want to win in a positive way. We call that electioneering instead of honest, fair reporting....And we're mad as hell at the way you never stop finding fault with our country."

Limbaugh and groups such as AIM have mounted a steady and loud barrage against the news media. They found a receptive audience among news consumers whose opinions about the media differed considerably from most journalists' perceptions of themselves.

This dichotomy of opinion was documented by (among others) the Times Mirror Center for The People and The Press during the 1992 campaign. One finding of a Times Mirror survey: "While 80 percent of the news media sample rated the '92 coverage as either good or excellent, surveys of the public throughout the campaign found fewer than six in ten rating press coverage of the campaign positively and more than one in three voters feeling that the press was doing only a fair or poor job."

Many journalists, it should be noted, are not sanguine about their professional behavior. For example, one ex-reporter says he quit the business because, "I could not spend the rest of my life producing the shallow, sensational, trumped-up trivia that passes for news today."[33]

Even those journalists of more moderate temperament realize that the news business is under siege. David Broder of *The Washington Post* writes, "People curse the messengers, even as they hungrily consume the message."[34]

Politicians also were unhappy with news coverage, especially the tendency of reporters to home in on the sensational and trivial while ignoring matters of substance. For instance, during the spring of 1992, the Clinton campaign's polling found voters were angry about the press's failure to provide background material they would need to cast an informed ballot. Some people, the polls showed, trusted information less when it came from the media.[35]

So, for all the pronouncements about the press as arbiter of voters' decision making, the public was sometimes inclined to take the politician's word over that of the reporter. And candidates realized that if they wanted to deliver a serious message about an issue, they'd be better off doing it through paid advertising rather than counting on the news media to present it to voters. Ross Perot was the most notable exponent of this approach, but even candidates with smaller bankrolls knew that they had to circumvent a news media establishment that was decreasingly credible.

News coverage procedures became more controversial in 1992 because of the unusual influence of print and television tabloid journalism. Discussing the "character issue" frenzy that dominated the campaign's early months, media critic Ken Auletta wrote: "(The tabloids) established the peer pressure. They set the pace. And they did it by relying more on rumor than reported fact."[36]

The state of the news business is important to Limbaugh because it affects the context in which he works. As public trust of traditional news sources diminishes, the voices of Limbaugh and other "new news" exponents have a better chance to be heard.

Accusations that major news organizations are biased are nothing new. The debate goes back and forth. In 1992, for instance, the conventional wisdom as the campaign ended was that news coverage had tilted in Clinton's favor. Of course, the counter-argument is that coverage of Gennifer Flowers's allegations and Clinton's Vietnam-era draft status had almost knocked the candidate out of the race.

Also, despite all the talk about "the liberal media," Republicans usually receive most of the editorial endorsements. From 1944 through 1988, the only Democratic presidential nominee to receive a plurality of newspaper endorsements was Lyndon Johnson in 1964. In terms of circulation, Republicans benefit even more: about 70 percent of the national daily newspaper audience reads newspapers endorsing Republicans.[37]

At least as important as purported partisan biases is the perception of exclusionary bias—that major news organizations are so intent on staying apace with the latest cultural fads (such as political correctness) that they forsake traditional values when deciding what is newsworthy and praiseworthy.

About this, Limbaugh says: "Most of the people of this country already have strong moral values. They're not represented in the mainstream media, where things people believe are made fun of. Most people feel that moral decay is at the root of all the ills we have in society."

That terse analysis indicates why Limbaugh is so popular. Like Ronald Reagan, he has an acute understanding of the American psyche. "Where things people believe are made fun of." A lot of people are angry about that, and they take seriously the country's moral decay. But, they think, try getting that message across to those smart-aleck, liberal journalists on the Sunday morning talk shows.

With the traditional news media in disfavor, a vacuum exists in the information delivery system. Rush Limbaugh fills at least part of that vacuum.

MEGADITTOS, RUSH

"He's saying what needs to be said."

"He's saying what I think."

Talk to Limbaugh fans, gathered in Rush Rooms or on their own, and those are comments you'll hear frequently. From seventy-five-year-old retirees and twenty-year-old college students. "Megadittos, Rush."

Even those who consider Limbaugh's approach to most issues to be biased and simplistic must be impressed with the devotion and explosive growth of his following. In the House of

Representatives, Democratic staff members monitor his broadcasts and prepare responses to his attacks. The Clinton White House is worried, too. According to one administration strategist, the Democrats are overmatched: "We, the Democrats generally, the liberals generally, do not have anything that rivals Rush Limbaugh. It's pretty pathetic. He's playing rollerball, and we're playing chess."[38]

Not only do many millions listen or watch Limbaugh every day, but millions also are paying for the privilege of imbibing his wisdom from his books, newsletters, tapes, and so on. He keeps his appeal fresh by limiting his reliance on his standard shtick; each day's news provides plenty of virgin material.

The news wires provide the raw substance that his showmanship molds into marketable commodity. He is part entertainer, with Bob Hope's timing, and part politician, with Ronald Reagan's instinct about what people want to hear.

He knows the game he's playing. He says: "You turn on the radio for three things:

entertainment, entertainment, entertainment. I'm in the business of drawing a crowd and then holding them."[39]

But while he entertains his crowds, he also sees himself—and his fans see him—as the agent for those who consider themselves "conservative" (which means different things to different people) at a time when conservatism's prospects seem shakier than they have in many years.

RUSH TO THE RESCUE

3

Limbaugh's popularity is best evaluated from two perspectives. First, looking at Limbaugh as political guru—an influential ideologue championing Reagan-Republican conservatism. Second, as entertainer—a master of the electronic media.

In this chapter and the next, the political side.

Rush Limbaugh was thirteen years old when Barry Goldwater mounted his ill-fated presidential campaign against Lyndon Johnson. In the conservative Limbaugh household and in conservative Cape Girardeau, the Arizona senator's pronouncements found more favor than they did in most of the rest of the country. But young Rush was then more interested in radio than politics, and certainly wasn't contemplating his eventual role as Barry Goldwater's ideological descendant.

Goldwater says that the 1964 campaign was not the beginning of a conservative revolution " because for most of our history the majority of Americans have considered themselves conservatives. They have often not voted that way because they were offered no clear choice." Goldwater notes that he, and later Ronald Reagan to much greater effect, tapped into a large, existing reservoir of conservatism.

In his memoirs, Goldwater cites approvingly some analysis by *The Washington Post*'s David Broder: "There's no question but that Barry Goldwater contributed to enormous political change in the country...Goldwater changed the country's political axis not only geographically but in terms of values and beliefs. He introduced modern conservative thought to the national debate....His race is also of the greatest importance because, despite Goldwater's loss, his campaign saw the greatest recruiting in the past generation."

Broder added that the press had under-estimated Goldwater's impact: "We missed the enormous significance...of what he was saying and his political effects on the country and the Republican Party....We missed where American politics was headed."[1]

Most in the news media have been similarly slow to take Limbaugh seriously. Perhaps this is because his mix of politics and entertainment makes him hard to categorize. Maybe he doesn't represent a change in the direction in which American politics is headed, but his popularity is evidence that a large conservative base remains intact. The ideological continuum that ran from Goldwater to Reagan—wavering according to the electoral vicissitudes of the moment—has continued on to Limbaugh.

Goldwater is still remembered for a few words in the speech he gave when accepting the Republican nomination in 1964: "Extremism in the defense of liberty is no vice, and...moderation in the pursuit of justice is no virtue." That line was offered by Democrats as proof that Goldwater condoned extremism in all its ugly manifestations.

That perception was a factor in his landslide defeat—he won only fifty-two electoral votes and just 39 percent of the popular vote. For years thereafter, Goldwater was regarded by many as something of a joke. His campaign was generally referred to as a "debacle" and was seen as a devastating—perhaps fatal—setback to the Republican Party and conservatism.

Of course, four years later that same Republican Party elected a president. And the conservative movement—less visible for a while— continued to grow stronger.

Goldwater gets only passing mention in *The Way Things Ought to Be*. Limbaugh credits Reagan as the one who "brought conservatism into the mainstream of the nation's political thought" and made sure that it would no longer be considered "a fringe, extreme, or reactionary movement."

Perhaps Limbaugh is making a shrewd judgment about whom to claim as political ancestor. Goldwater had lost and his politics had been equated to extremist folly. Reagan, on the other hand, was a winner, worthy of emulation.

Despite the glitzy rhetoric, Limbaugh rarely strays far from the mainstream, and tries to avoid crossing into extremism. Clearly, he knows what happens to commentators who are perceived as nuts: they don't find air time on six hundred stations or earn millions of dollars.

Of course, Goldwater, of all people, understood the disastrous consequences of being perceived as dwelling on the lunatic fringe. By 1988, when he wrote his memoirs, he was ready to offer cautionary words about extremism that Limbaugh might take to heart. He criticizes what he sees as the tendency of the New Right to stress "the politics of absolute moral right and wrong," and says, "the GOP will be weakened if it adopts the exclusionary views of the religious right."[2]

That is Goldwater as born-again pragmatist. As such, he shares some ground with Limbaugh.

A NEW CONSERVATISM

In the aftermath of the Goldwater defeat, political historian Theodore H. White wrote, "There is still room in America for a new creation of the conservative imagination to reorder the growing complexity of American life. Barry Goldwater signally failed to deliver this conservative vision in 1964, offering little more than a Populism of the right."[3]

To follow the Johnson-Nixon-Ford-Carter years, conservatives reemerged with a candidate far stronger but no less controversial than Goldwater—Ronald Reagan. Theodore White again: "His fervor was unfeigned—the fervor of a man consumed by ideas. His were simple ideas, to be sure, but they more vividly repudiated the dominant ideas of his time than those of any other candidate since Barry Goldwater."[4]

Reagan is frequently cited by Limbaugh in *The Way Things Ought to Be*. In fact, Limbaugh says he shortened his chapter, "Ronald Reagan: Setting Things Straight," because he had discussed Reagan in so many other places throughout the book. Because of these frequent mentions, Limbaugh tells his readers, "it should be obvious to you how important I deem Ronald Reagan to have been in shaping the future course of this nation, and indeed the world."[5]

Writing about Reagan's 1966 election as governor of California as an indicator of the meaning of his 1980 campaign, Harvard professor James Q. Wilson argues that he was not a mere product of "Hollywood eccentricities," but rather was much more an issues-oriented politician. He was, said Wilson, rooted in a political culture "that was concerned, not with ideology but with property, not with some romantic vision of the past but with a desire for a future in which rewards would be allocated on the basis of effort, decency, and competence."

His supporters, continued Wilson, "thought that right living based on traditional values would produce a good society and were in rebellion against what they took to be the efforts of some to acquire benefits without effort or to debase society by wrong living." Reagan, added Wilson, "is at once a candidate for the Presidency and the spokesman of a social movement."[6]

In White's and Wilson's analyses of Reagan can be seen the roots of Limbaugh's attraction to Reagan as conservative avatar, as "a man to whom we Americans owe a debt that we will never be able to repay." Limbaugh is unabashedly worshipful: "I couldn't submit an issues-oriented book for publication without paying tribute to Mr. Reagan, and crediting him with the phenomenal difference he made in our future and that of our children."

Reagan owed much of his influence to his skill as "the great communicator," and to his perceived kinship with his followers. In 1959, Vice President Richard Nixon wrote a letter to actor Ronald Reagan, who was dabbling in politics. Nixon noted, "You have the ability of putting complicated technical ideas into words everyone can understand. Those of us who have spent a number of years in Washington too often lack the ability to express ourselves in this way."[7]

Journalist Richard Reeves made a similar observation about Reagan a quarter century later: "He held a set of simple beliefs and was able to express them in simple and direct language. He did not sound like a politician, which made him a great politician.[8]

And in 1980, when asked about his appeal to voters, Reagan answered: "Would you laugh if I told you that I think maybe they see themselves and that I'm one of them? I've never been able to detach myself or think that I, somehow, am apart from them."[9]

Limbaugh's career history has similarities to Reagan's. Both sons of the Midwest, they began their careers at small radio stations and they found success in California in the communications industry. Limbaugh well understands the Reagan communication skills and the Reagan mystique. Like Reagan, Limbaugh uses "words everyone can understand" (unlike a conservative commentator of similar viewpoint, but different style, William F. Buckley). Limbaugh also appreciates how Reagan "made people understand that they're not insignificant in the functioning of the great institutions of the country. Reagan made people feel good about themselves....Reagan awakened their confidence."[10]

But Limbaugh's success is due not merely to Reagan-like stylistic flourishes. Just as Reagan himself was much more a man of issues than most of his critics acknowledge, Limbaugh thinks about what he is saying. Even apparently glib remarks are grounded in Limbaugh's interpretation of conservatism. For example, when he rails against the Clinton administration's proposed health-care reforms and says there is no health crisis, his premise is that whatever changes take place in health care should not be the province of the federal government. He is opposed not to better health care, but to Washington-dominated policy and regulation.

Reagan broadened and redefined the appeal of conservatism. He reinvigorated the conservative tradition and the conservative constituency. And when he left the White House he left behind a strong political force that George Bush was unable to understand or harness, but that Limbaugh skillfully presides over as one of Reagan's heirs.

THE REAGAN CONNECTION

Some dismiss Ronald Reagan as merely a perpetuator of illusions; at best, "the faded idol as reachable ideal." But even critics are warily respectful of him and his hold on America's political imagination. "He wrests from us something warmer than mere popularity, a kind of complicity....Reagan does not argue for American values; he embodies them."[11]

Some critical descriptions of Reagan are strikingly similar to those of Limbaugh, particularly those noting how both men's influence was underestimated. Limbaugh has been dismissed by irritated liberals as an inconsequential blowhard whose nasty jokes couldn't possibly find a large audience. Such comments are not unlike the pronouncements before the 1980 presidential campaign that no one would vote for a has-been movie actor for president.

Texas journalist Ronnie Dugger has this to say about Reagan: "No ordinary person could have achieved what Reagan has. When it counted he was underestimated by his natural adversaries the liberals, initially in California during his first run for the governorship, then in 1980 throughout the country. They thought he was just an actor, and not too bright. In fact, he is a serious right-wing ideologue, he is a mesmerizing speaker, he is tactically resilient and opportunistic, and he is smart....His style is free of self-doubt."[12]

Change a few words, and you'll have a pretty good description of Rush Limbaugh.

Some of Reagan's and Limbaugh's public utterances also have much in common. For instance, in his 1985 State of the Union message, Reagan said, "Four years ago, we began to change—forever, I hope—our assumptions about government and its place in our lives." In this speech and in many other pronouncements, Reagan distinguished between 'America' and 'government,' praising the former while attacking the latter. Limbaugh often does the same thing.

An example: Reagan and Limbaugh remarks about welfare. (The Reagan comment comes, appropriately, from a pre-presidential radio broadcast.)

> *Reagan*: "Welfare is a dangerous drug destroying the spirit of people once proudly independent. Our mission should be to help people kick that particular drug habit."

> *Limbaugh*: "Some people are raised to believe they are incapable of achieving anything unless government helps them...through welfare programs, which destroy their self-reliance."

In both instances, *people* are victimized by unwise *government*.

Itemized parallels are not as important as is Limbaugh's overall perpetuation of Reagan-style conservatism. In his speech accepting the Republican nomination in 1980, Reagan endorsed a "community of values embodied in these words: family, work, neighborhood, peace, and freedom."

Limbaugh sees himself as champion of this same community of values and follows Reagan's lead in using rhetoric that some might consider corny. Limbaugh, like Reagan, will talk about families and neighborhoods with an ardor that soon has radio listeners seeing Norman Rockwell's America in their minds' eye.

Presidential scholar Hugh Heclo noted: "Just as liberalism made it all right to talk about sex, Reaganism made it all right to talk about patriotism, work requirements and family values, parochial allegiances, moral purpose and, yes, imposing middle-class values on others. Reaganism has a future because Americans want to talk about these things in politics." Along the same lines, political scientist John Kenneth White argues that the true Reagan legacy "lies not so much in his actions as president, but in the 'sense of return' he has given the American people in their values."[13]

Many of Reagan's homilies are characterized by a softer edge than the one Limbaugh hones on his commentaries. At the 1992 Republican National Convention, for instance, Reagan's address was notable first because it was the best written of any at that GOP gathering (certainly better than the acceptance speech of his successor, George Bush). His words rolled forth in his familiar cadence: "We were meant to be masters of destiny, not victims of fate."

And he offered this valedictory: "Whatever else history may say about me when I'm gone, I hope it will record that I appealed to your best hopes, not your worst fears; to your confidence rather than your doubts."

Those words stood in marked contrast to the bitter convention rhetoric of Pat Buchanan, Rich Bond, and others who were intent on appealing to fears rather than hopes.

In his radio monologues about the policy crisis of the moment, Limbaugh often falls between the two. Although his humor usually keeps him from drifting into overt nastiness, he lacks the above-it-all gentleness Reagan displayed in his convention speech. Limbaugh has a tricky tightrope to walk. He doesn't want his comments to lose their bite and audience appeal, nor does he want to be perceived as mean-spirited. Even many of his devoted fans would eventually find that tiresome. His critics are already convinced he likes nothing more than to flaunt his total disrespect for those individuals or groups he doesn't agree with.

As candidate and president, Reagan had mastered the subtleties of mood. In 1980, he benefited when compared to the often dour Jimmy Carter. According to Theodore H. White: "In a season of melancholy his good nature pleased. The camera stimulates Reagan as catnip does a cat; he loves, as a television personality does, the one-line quip."[14]

Limbaugh is likewise stimulated by the camera or microphone, and is likewise ready to skewer a politician or issue with a crisp one-liner (often followed by a mini-sermon). He is getting better at letting his good-natured side prevail over his mean streak. Perhaps as a product of his growing confidence, his self-deprecating humor shines through more often.

Reagan in his 1984 campaign, "had framed the election as a choice between not merely two programs for governing America but two general moods, or temperamental inclinations—'optimism' on the Republican side and 'pessimism' on the Democratic side."[15] He did not always "convey a clear vision of the technological present nor of the mechanistically defined future, but he conveyed a vision of America. It was a vision more of pride than of purpose. But perhaps pride was the purpose."[16] This was a pride in self—in being American.

His television advertising during the '84 race captured this notion. Soft-focus portraits of idyllic communities illustrated the theme, "It's morning again in America."

Occasionally, Limbaugh displays a similarly gentle touch. And, like Reagan, he possesses the timing and delivery of a natural showman. But he has yet to establish himself as a reassuring figure like his idol. As *Time*'s William A. Henry has observed, Reagan possessed an "almost uniquely potent weapon: he was not merely respected or feared but liked." Limbaugh is respected (sometimes grudgingly) and perhaps feared by political foes. But liked? Despite his occasional attempts at sounding avuncular, he certainly was not liked as Reagan was liked (perhaps adored) by a broad spectrum of conservatives. Maybe it will yet come.

TAKING THE TORCH

As ideologue, Limbaugh picked up the torch that he considered to have been dropped by George Bush, whose own conservatism often seemed more a matter of convenience than belief. Referring to Bush as "the pastel president," George Will writes, "no politician was ever more passive clay in the hands of handlers than Bush was in 1988."[17]

Will described "Bushism" as "feel-good politics, adding self-satisfaction to the material comfort of the comfortable. It is highly popular and applicable to any issue." That kind of politics is far removed from the ideological crusade of Reaganism. Limbaugh, too, is made of sterner stuff.

Will also criticized Bush's sense of political purpose: "Some people seek office to be something; others seek office to do something. Bush is one of the former. In this, the contrast with Ronald Reagan is complete."[18]

Limbaugh has never been as critical of Bush as George Will has, but in the midst of the 1992 campaign, Limbaugh had a message for the president: "If I could say anything to George Bush, it would be this: 'Mr. President, the people of this country desperately want you to be and do what you said you were going to do in 1988. They would love to vote for you. And you can still do it, you can make them feel that way. It's going to take an incredible amount of passion, because passion right now is the only thing that's going to make you believable, because there are too many legitimate doubts about your lip-service to these things that elected you in the first place.'"

At the root of Limbaugh's uneasiness about Bush was the distinction between broad-based Reaganism and traditional upper-class conservatism. Limbaugh is loyal to the former; Bush is a product of the latter.

Especially in domestic policy, the Bush presidency was merely a holding action. According to *Time*'s Michael Duffy and Dan Goodgame—veteran Bush-watchers—Bush is "deeply conservative in his fear of change, his skepticism toward government's attempts to promote social progress, his caution and reactiveness. When faced with a decision, Bush often concluded that the best course was to do as little as possible: to 'do no harm,' rather than attempt reform at the risk of making things worse."

Reagan as president certainly was conservative, but—like Barry Goldwater—more of a radical conservative than Bush was. He was a crusader, willing—sometimes eager—to take chances for the good of the cause. Bush, on the other hand, "fears change and distrusts crusades," preferring to defend the status quo. Duffy and Goodgame say, "In his fundamental attitudes toward change, progress, established institutions, and hierarchies, and the established role of government, Bush is far more conservative than Reagan."

That, however, is not Limbaugh's kind of conservatism, nor did it have much appeal to the hard-right activists in the Republican Party. Conservatives of this ilk "had never liked, nor trusted, Bush. Reagan was their candidate, and everyone else was just a cheap imitation."[19]

Unhappy about Bush's abandonment of his "no new taxes" pledge, Limbaugh urged New Hampshire voters to support GOP challenger Patrick Buchanan in their state's primary. Buchanan was delighted. He promised—who knows how seriously—to make Limbaugh the communications chief in the Buchanan White House.

Limbaugh later said of his backing Buchanan: "That was my effort to send the president a message. The Republican Party and George Bush got in trouble when they moved to the left, when they signed on with the civil rights bill with its quotas, and the tax increases. He let down people who elected him. And so he then attracts the Wimp II image."[20]

After Buchanan embarrassed Bush by winning sixty-five thousand votes—37 percent of the total—in New Hampshire, the Bush team decided to co-opt Limbaugh. The talk show host was not able to resist the president's charm, especially since he was exposed to it while an overnight guest at the White House. Finding enough in common with Bush to tilt heavily his way during the campaign, Limbaugh helped rally unenthusiastic Republicans behind the GOP ticket. He even waived his "no guests" policy and had both Bush and Vice President Dan Quayle on his show.

But even this chumminess didn't dispel Limbaugh's unhappiness about Bush's lack of ideological fervor. Conservatives who had formed loyal ranks behind Reagan's leadership now were drifting. They remembered how Bush in 1980 had trashed their hero's economic plan as "voodoo economics" and they saw Bush's tax hike compromise as betrayal of the cause.

Even in 1984, during his second go-round on Reagan's ticket, Bush had seemed unwilling to line up behind the president's cleverly worded position on taxes. Reagan had said, "We have no plans for, nor will I allow any plans for, a tax increase." To that, Bush unhelpfully added that because economic conditions could change, "any president would keep his options open." Reporters, probing for a possible schism between the two men, elicited a particularly odd piece of always-odd Bushian rhetoric in response to their questions: "No more nit-picking. Zippity doo-dah! Now it's off to the races."[21] No wonder Reagan loyalists weren't sure exactly where Bush stood.

In some quarters, Bush was the object of constant suspicion. For example, even his acceptance speech at the 1988 Republican National

Convention—a speech deemed by many to be the best of his career—irritated some Reaganites. If Bush was promising "a kinder, gentler nation," he must mean that the nation under Reagan wasn't kind or gentle enough. How dare he?

And when Bush moved into the White House, some members of his staff went out of their way to tell reporters that this would be a more intellectual and effective presidency than that of doddering old Ronnie. That arrogance didn't win many friends among conservatives loyal to Reagan.

LOYALTY TO REAGAN

Despite Bush's expedience-dictated efforts to appear a Reagan clone in the eyes of the GOP right wing, he never was wholly successful at doing so. In the differences between Reagan's conservatism and Bush's faux-conservatism lie the reasons for Limbaugh's steadfast devotion to Reagan and fluctuating support for Bush.

That is how Limbaugh's flirtation with Buchanan evolved. It was not a declaration of allegiance to Buchanan as much as it was an affirmation of continued loyalty to Reaganism.

Here also can be found the roots of Limbaugh's emergence as influential leader of the Reaganist renaissance among conservative Republican ideologues.

CONSERVATIVES IN DISARRAY: THE 1992 ELECTION

4

In 1992's final field of three candidates, George Bush clearly was Limbaugh's favorite. But despite the public displays of mutual affection—with passion increasing as election day drew closer—little real affinity existed between the two men. Limbaugh the ideologue was put off by Bush's philosophical vacuousness. Bush's noblesse oblige could not obscure his mistrust of a zealot.

To firm up his standing as a fiscal conservative, Bush had keyed his 1988 campaign to a Reaganesque promise about taxes that he made in his convention speech: "I'm the one who won't raise taxes...My opponent won't rule out raising taxes. But I will. The Congress will push me to raise taxes, and I'll say no, and they'll push, and I'll say no, and they'll push again. And all I can say to them is, Read my lips: no new taxes."

This rhetoric was part of Bush's continuing attempt to build bridges to Reagan conservatives. His efforts suffered a major setback when Republican National Chairman Lee Atwater died of brain cancer in 1991. Atwater, a protégé of South Carolina senator Strom Thurmond, understood the wariness about Bush and had begun in the mid-1980s to target key conservative leaders and events for Bush to visit.

Without Atwater, Bush had no one to guide him reliably through the minefield of conservative sensitivities. Although his White House chief of staff, former New Hampshire governor John Sununu, had good conservative credentials, he didn't have the political sense needed to orchestrate diplomatic maneuvers such as those Atwater had launched.

When events were working in his favor—most notably, the Persian Gulf War—Bush's approval ratings remained spectacularly high. The war distracted people from economic worries, and the Democrats were in their usual disarray, unable to articulate appealing opposition policy positions.

But Bush had only a fragile mandate. For much of his presidency, Bush remained politically adrift, out of touch with reality among Republicans and the rest of the electorate. This sloppiness became strikingly obvious even before the 1992 campaign formally got underway.

The preliminaries to campaign '92 began in 1991, and despite the macho glow of the Gulf War victory, Bush's prospective vulnerability became apparent. In a special U.S. Senate election in Pennsylvania (to fill the seat of air-crash victim John Heinz), Bush's attorney general, Richard Thornburgh, was upset by Democrat Harris Wofford. Early polls had shown Thornburgh leading by forty points, but Wofford hammered away at economic and health care issues, coupled with attacks on the Washington establishment. He won comfortably, and on election night claimed that his victory marked the beginning of the end of the Bush administration.

Thornburgh's defeat was unsettling, but the more serious damage to Bush had been done the year before. On June 26, 1990, Bush issued a statement admitting that "tax revenue increases" would be required as part of a budget package. After previously holding fast to his "read my lips" pledge, this reversal was sudden, lacking any preliminary public relations maneuvers that might have lessened the shock value of the change. Republican strategist Jim Lake said that this failure to "lay a foundation" illustrated a significant flaw in the Bush White House: "They never really understood the essential need...that the president must convey to the American people his thoughts of where he's taking the country."

Conservatives were livid. Ed Rollins, who later defected (briefly) to the Perot campaign, said Bush's move was "probably the most serious violation of any political pledge anybody has ever made."[1]

The issue wasn't just economic policy. It was honesty, credibility. He had made a promise that helped elect him in 1988, and now he'd broken it. Why should anyone believe him about anything? The Democrats understood the potency of this, and delightedly used the "read my lips" quote in their campaign advertising.

Bush was clearly stumbling as he entered 1992. The tax deal had badly damaged his credibility. Public memories of Gulf War glory were being erased by a stubborn recession, and the Pennsylvania election showed that the Democrats were still alive.

The President was increasingly a mere cipher as far as conservatives were concerned. Even Ronald Reagan was apparently fed up with his successor. In February, Bush went to California to call on the former president, obviously hoping for a helpful media event that would signal conservatives especially that Bush, not Buchanan, had Reagan's stamp of approval.

But on the day of the visit, the *Washington Post* ran a story quoting Reagan as saying, "Bush doesn't seem to stand for anything." At Reagan's house, the press corps was kept outside the grounds and the fence was shrouded in brown paper to prevent any Bush-Reagan photos from being taken.[2] The message from Reagan was clear.

All this worked to create a vacuum. Reagan was disinheriting Bush. Buchanan's politics might have been fine, but his strident nastiness made him unappealing. So who was left? Perhaps there was no one else to vote for, but there was someone who seemed to conservatives to be truly one of their own: the self-described "epitome of morality and virtue," Rush Limbaugh.

Of course, being responsible for delivering wisdom rather than enacting policy gave Limbaugh an inherent advantage over Bush and all other politicians. Limbaugh, for example, could endorse a "no new taxes" pledge and never have to worry about steering a budget package through Congress. In other words, Limbaugh was living the politician's dream: having authority without responsibility.

This dichotomy between hard political reality and Limbaugh's more cushioned political world did not seem to bother Limbaugh's audience. Throughout 1992, his listenership grew. The same factors that were to produce such a large voter turnout in November were contributing to Limbaugh's rising ratings. People wanted answers. Rush provided them.

THE BUSH DOWNFALL

George Bush had problems far greater than conservative disaffection. The nuts and bolts of his campaign hadn't come together. Good speeches weren't being written, good ads weren't being produced, smart strategy wasn't being planned. The well-oiled machine that had chewed up Michael Dukakis four years before was nowhere in evidence.

Add to this Ross Perot's feisty campaigning, which was winning the loyalty of voters who liked their candidates to be as similar to John Wayne as possible. The Bush camp never did decide whether Perot should be courted, attacked, or ignored.

But the biggest problems Bush faced were the revived Democratic Party and its smart, tough nominee. They would make Limbaugh an even more important player.

In 1985, Congresswoman Pat Schroeder joked: "There are three things the Democratic Party must do to win the White House. Unfortunately, no one knows what they are."[3] For Schroeder's fellow Democrats, that was as sad as it was funny, especially since the line remained accurate year after year.

Their party seemed incapable of winning a presidential race, despite its almost perpetual control of both houses of Congress and its solid performance in state and local elections. By 1992, except for Jimmy Carter's win, the drought had lasted twenty-eight years—since Lyndon Johnson's victory in 1964. After Bush had overcome a fifteen-point deficit in the polls to defeat Michael Dukakis in 1988, Democrats began believing those pundits who said the Republican tide would run at least until the end of the century.

Democratic nominees such as George McGovern, Walter Mondale, and Dukakis had been damaged by being labeled "liberals." They tended to handle the charge badly, often denying it without anyone ever clearly understanding what the purported intrinsic evil of liberalism was.

Despite the intellectual emptiness of the charge, Republican strategists used it effectively. For many voters, liberalism was a code word signaling free spending and moral permissiveness. The middle-class whites who make up much of the crucial swing vote in presidential elections thought the Democrats ran roughshod over their needs and desires while catering to racial minorities, the poor, and the elite white liberals who ran the party.[4]

In the skilled hands of Republican pols such as Lee Atwater, James Baker, and Roger Ailes, this perception had been a powerful weapon. Joining the fray, Limbaugh constantly described liberalism

as a lazy person's politics that required no thinking, just knee-jerk reaction. Affirmative action,
banning school prayer, gun control—these were
among the issues, said Limbaugh, that would get
the liberal wolf pack baying.

Some pragmatic Democratic leaders realized that rather than wasting time in disputes about
semantics they would be better off accepting the
fact that voters didn't want to cast a presidential
ballot for a liberal. If they want something else,
give them something else.

That's not easily done. "Conservative
Democrat" is an oxymoron, regardless of some politicians' eagerness to wear the label. And anyway, if
people want a conservative, they'll vote Republican
and know they're more likely to get the real thing.

"Moderate" is ambiguous; just about
anyone can claim to be a moderate. It is nicely
non-threatening, promising calm political waters.
To some Democratic leaders emerging from
shell-shock induced by the 1984 Reagan landslide,
the middle ground looked like the place to be.

In 1985, the Democratic Leadership Council was born, with founding members including Senators Charles Robb of Virginia and Sam Nunn of Georgia, and Governor Bill Clinton of Arkansas. (Jesse Jackson dubbed the group, "the Southern White Boy Caucus" and "Democrats for the Leisure Class.") They promised "to lead the Democratic Party back to the political mainstream and restore America's sense of national purpose." These "new Democrats," said the DLC's promotional material, "don't want to lead America right or left. They want to move the country forward."

Beyond such innocuous claims was an edging away from New Deal-like government activism and a recognition that many voters thought Democrats could not be trusted in the White House. Democratic pollster Celinda Lake told party officials in 1990 that the middle class remained unconvinced of the Democrats' fiscal responsibility. "People don't feel the Democrats understand that taxes are real money," she said. "They think (that the Democrats believe) it is Monopoly money."[5] This is a theme that Limbaugh uses frequently to deride the Democrats.

Responding to such concerns, the DLC emphasized fiscal restraint and middle-class values, urging state governments to devise innovative ways to supplant federal initiatives, enhancing competitiveness through government-labor-business partnerships, and using market-based incentives to help the poor.[6]

Some liberals say this DLC agenda is just "Republican Lite," and sells out the constituencies—such as the poor and minorities—that have traditionally supported, and counted on support from, the Democratic Party. Among the party's liberals are those who think that "winning elections is not worth changing the party's historical principles, that any deviation from party orthodoxy, even to deal with a changing society, is unacceptable." Some of these Democrats "see adapting to a new era as treasonous instead of smart."[7]

Despite intraparty feuding, the pragmatists prevailed in 1992. This recasting of the Democrats' public persona helped work electoral magic. As he contemplated his run for the White House, Bill Clinton understood that the Reagan legacy would outlive George Bush's bungling. The values of Reaganism could be expected to remain the values of a majority of those who voted.

Although Bill Clinton and Rush Limbaugh would be loath to admit any kind of kinship to each other, they both have found success by embracing work ethic, patriotism, family, and other values that the middle class takes more seriously than the Democratic Party has in recent years.

Consider this message in a fund-raising letter: "Our country is in trouble—and it's up to you and me to do something about it. The Washington insiders won't do it. We sent them to Washington to make things better. Instead, they're only making matters worse. The hour is late. The clock is ticking." And about a specific issue—welfare—the letter says: "There are two problems with our welfare system. One, it does more to keep the poor on welfare than to help them get off. Two, it no longer reflects the values that money can't buy: honesty, responsibility, and the dignity of work."

All that sounds as if Rush Limbaugh, or perhaps Ronald Reagan, had written it. But it was sent over the signature of U.S. Senator John Breaux of Louisiana, Clinton's successor as head of the DLC, in November 1991. It illustrates how the rising moderate wing of the party wanted to approach the 1992 campaign.

The vast middle class was the target. They are the people who make or break candidates. In his convention acceptance speech, Clinton said, "I am a product of the middle class, and when I am president you will be forgotten no more."

CLINTON MOVES RIGHT

Clinton, like Limbaugh, understands that many Americans respond to symbols that represent the values they consider important. For instance, support of the death penalty symbolizes a tough anti-crime stance. In 1988, Bush repeatedly attacked Dukakis for being soft on crime, and the

Democratic nominee's opposition to the death penalty was seen as substantiation of Bush's charge.

In 1992, Clinton took that issue away from the Republicans. He endorsed capital punishment, and at one point in the campaign made a well-publicized trip to Arkansas to oversee the execution of a state prison inmate. (The fact that the prisoner was brain-damaged attracted little attention.)

Clinton doesn't go as far as Limbaugh does on this issue. On his radio show, Limbaugh has approvingly referred to executed prisoners as having "assumed room temperature." But few voters need such extreme rhetoric. They just want reassurance that their president will protect their interests over those of the criminals. On this and similar issues, a Limbaugh-vs.-Dukakis struggle would have been far more fiery than battling Clinton. For Limbaugh, as for Bush, Clinton as campaigner proved to be a difficult-to-hit target. (As president, Clinton has turned out to be far easier for Limbaugh to clobber.)

Arms-length treatment of Jesse Jackson was another example of Clinton's moving closer to Limbaugh's world view than to that of Democratic liberals. For reasons rooted in race, Jackson evokes fear and dislike from many people, especially the "Reagan-Bush Democrats" who had been so important in keeping Republicans in the White House, and whose backing Clinton so desperately needed to have.

In 1988, Dukakis had thought he had unified the party by negotiating with Jackson and letting him play a dominant role at the party's national convention. But many voters saw this as just another Democratic sell-out to the most liberal of special interests.

Clinton wasn't about to let that happen. He made it a point to exclude Jackson from the 1991 Democratic Leadership Council convention, and was unperturbed when Jackson loudly criticized the DLC. More significantly, he picked a fight with Jackson in the middle of the 1992 campaign. The incident he seized on was a minor one—a comment by a little-known entertainer—but the message Clinton sent was clear: when forced to choose between the Left and the Middle, Clinton was going to stick with the Middle.

A rap singer known as Sister Souljah had defended the violence of the Los Angeles riots and in an interview had asked: "If black people kill black people every day, why not have a week and kill white people?...If you're a gang member and you normally would be killing somebody, why not kill a white person?"

Although few Americans other than rap fans had ever heard of Sister Souljah, her comments raised an issue that had been devastating to Democrats in past elections. Rather than condemning her advocacy of violence, the prototypical Democrat would try to excuse it, citing the terrible social conditions from which violence arose. Some voters might consider that approach enlightened, but many others would think it the worst kind of pandering. It would be the "typical Democratic cowardice" that Limbaugh and the GOP would loudly excoriate.

Sister Souljah had been given a forum by Jesse Jackson's Rainbow Coalition. When Clinton later appeared before the coalition—with Jackson sitting beside him—he chastised its members for apparently condoning remarks "filled with hatred." He added, "If you took the words 'white' and 'black' and reversed them, you might think David Duke was giving that speech."

Jackson was visibly angry. He later called a press conference to defend Sister Souljah and criticize Clinton.

As all this played out on television, it amounted to a clear strategic gain for Clinton. Jesse Jackson was mad at him. To the Reagan-Bush Democrats, that was a plus for Clinton. He had come out against what appeared to be the sanctioning of anti-white violence by a rap singer. Consider which side of this issue the huge majority of middle-class white voters would come down on. Here was a Democrat standing up to Jackson. Good for him.

In seizing the moment, Clinton displayed well-calculated political timing a la Ronald Reagan.

Among party leaders and voters—particularly Southerners and blue collar workers—Clinton had scored. His claim to be a "different kind of Democrat" now meant something.

Limbaugh also criticized Sister Souljah, but no more strongly than Clinton did. Limbaugh also said: "Liberals and black leadership, instead of condoning this violence and blaming it on society, should be trying to build hope for the poor people in our inner cities. They should be seeking ways to wean them off the government dependency cycle and, quite frankly, from dependence on the self-serving black leadership."[8]

Much of that passage sounds like an excerpt from a Clinton speech.

Again, this isn't to say that these two men are ideological brothers. Rather, it shows that Clinton, like Limbaugh, was being pulled by the magnet of Reaganism. For political candidates and political commentators, this was the way to win votes and audience.

CIRCLING THE WAGONS

During the last months of the campaign, Limbaugh stood by George Bush, flawed though the president's conservatism might have been. Limbaugh was happy to dispense advice to Bush and take potshots at Clinton.

In an October 1992 article in *National Review*, Limbaugh counseled Bush about how to deal with Clinton. "To be reelected," he wrote, "Mr. Bush must unmask Bill Clinton and Al Gore as the liberals they really are." He suggested that the "liberal 'outing' of Clinton can be achieved in part by simply identifying Clinton's support base." He recited a list of the liberal special interest groups that he loathes and were supporting Clinton.

He also urged Bush to acknowledge his mistake in agreeing to the 1990 tax increases and to re-embrace supply-side policies. He wanted Bush to underscore the Democrat's attitude toward taxation: "Clinton *loves* raising taxes! He can't wait. Good grief, he has promised a $150-billion tax increase *before* he is elected. What will he do if people are ditzy enough to elect him on this basis?"

Another strategy suggestion was for Bush to "tie Bill Clinton to the tax-and-spend, corrupt Congress. He must transfer the congressional negatives to Clinton by demonstrating that Clinton is tied to Congress on most of the major issues, and is in collusion with them in opposing term limits....If the President succeeds in tying Clinton to Congress, and simultaneously in driving home Congress's low approval rating, he can run against both of them as a match made in hell."

Limbaugh's final point was that Bush "must present a vision of purpose and optimism"—the "vision thing" that Bush had always handled so awkwardly. The essence of this, said Limbaugh, was to assert the dominance of people over programs, individuals over government. This Reaganized libertarianism, Limbaugh argued, could carry the day for Bush.

In a mid-October *New York Times* op-ed piece, Limbaugh mounted a crisper defense of

Bush and attack on Clinton. Dismissing the Democrat as a "Robo-Candidate...whose most effective weapon is to stupefy voters," Limbaugh urged Bush to let his anger show. The key to the candidates' debates, wrote Limbaugh, "is television ability, pure and simple." Bush, he said, "must marshal his passion, his energy, his conviction, his confidence," particularly when explaining his optimism about the economy. But as he urged the president to "take off the gloves," Limbaugh sounded resigned to—as well as already indignant about—the predicted Election Day results.

CLINTON'S HOT SEAT

As candidate, Bill Clinton masterfully steered the treacherous course between his party's traditionalists and the "New Democrats" who wanted to jettison liberalism. He understood that the concerns of ideologues and voters are often different, and he had sense enough to favor the latter. Even the destabilizing presence of Ross Perot did not distract Clinton from his mission.

But once he moved into the White House in January 1993, his shrewd discipline seemed to vanish. The candidate who had kept resolutely focused on economic matters of interest to many now was ensnared in a liberal social agenda championed by few.

He became embroiled in debate about the role of homosexuals in the military, an issue reminiscent of the out-of-touch liberalism that had alienated voters during the failed campaigns of McGovern, Mondale, and Dukakis. After less than two weeks in office, he was flailing about, trying to pull public attention to his vague promises about welfare reform rather than leaving it focused on the gays in the military debate. (And Republicans kicked themselves for not having hammered Clinton about this gay-rights issue during the campaign.)

Clinton was giving Limbaugh all the ammunition he would need for months to come.

Neoconservative Democrat Ben Wattenberg, who had endorsed Clinton, said: "All the signals he is sending are to the opposite of what he conveyed in the campaign. It's worse than wrong; it's stupid."[9]

Much of the public perceived the first months of the Clinton presidency as being dedicated to a liberal agenda: tax hikes rather than spending cuts, dangerously expensive schemes about health care, endorsement of homosexuality, willingness to appoint radical or unqualified people to high posts, and so on. Some of the realities about these issues were different than the way the public saw them, but in politics perception is often as important as reality.

Clinton can take heart from knowing that eventually attitudes might change. For example, when Lani Guinier is long forgotten, Janet Reno might still be a major asset.

But for the short haul, at least, Clinton had alienated a large part of the base that had elected him. This wasn't just a matter of electoral dynamics. His presidency's high ambitions would be jeopardized without that base. Congress ignores the wishes of presidents who are judged to be politically wounded. As journalist John B. Judis observed, "No politician can hope to reform the economy without the firm support of middle-class voters, who must bear much of the sacrifice needed to address America's economic problems."

The middle class might have become disenchanted with Clinton, but they still had Rush Limbaugh to turn to.

"Rush, you're the only one out there who knows what's going on in the real world."

That was the message from a caller to the radio show in September 1993. He said he was a small businessman and fed up with government, banks, and things in general.

Immediately after the 1992 election, broadcast industry insiders speculated that Limbaugh's popularity would quickly fade. Without the daily controversy of a campaign, so the reasoning went, public interest in politics would be only sporadic—certainly not enough to sustain the Limbaugh empire.

Limbaugh had heard this before. He had begun his national radio show during the 1988 campaign, and, he noted, "They said I would have nothing to talk about after the election and for four years they've been saying I'm too controversial and too conservative."[10] They were wrong then, and the early-1993 ratings showed the doubters to be wrong again. In the twelve months ending with February 1993, Limbaugh's audience had grown 58 percent.

Even after four years of George Bush and the first months of the Clinton regime, Limbaugh's political thinking remains firmly anchored in the Reagan era. He prizes a note he received from Reagan that says: "Thanks for all you're doing to promote Republican and conservative principles. Now that I've retired from active politics, I don't mind that you've become the number-one voice for conservatism in our country. I know the liberals call you 'the most dangerous man in America,' but don't worry about it; they used to say the same thing about me. Keep up the good work. America needs to hear 'the way things ought to be.'"

Limbaugh takes that advice from Reagan seriously. He has said, "I have no interest in coexisting with liberals." Also, he laments the passing of the 1980s, because he sees the Reagan years as a golden age.

Some might think this is an odd way to view the Reagan presidency—ignoring the Iran-contra and savings and loan scandals, oblivious to the monstrous deficit for which Reaganomics was a growth potion, dismissing arguments about perpetuation of social inequities. Few historians would be so charitable, but that doesn't bother Limbaugh. Few historians reach as many people as he does. (In fact, probably no historian reaches even a tenth as large an audience as belongs to Limbaugh.)

Because he is not a candidate for anything— and has vowed not to become one—Limbaugh can be both above politics and very political. He's not asking for votes, so his credibility is easier to protect than that of an office-seeker. And by relying on Reaganism as the foundation on which he builds his commentaries about issues of the moment, he can maintain a consistency of outlook that eludes most candidates.

His basic thesis about the eighties is that Reagan limited government's ability to obstruct. "People tried to better themselves and for once there were fewer...obstacles in their way."

Limbaugh strikes out at the naysayers: "We are constantly reminded by the media how people spent profligately and consumed obscenely—how the rich got richer and the poor got poorer—under Reagan. Don't you believe it. Don't let the liberals deceive you into believing that a decade of sustained growth without inflation in America resulted in a bigger gap between the haves and the have-nots."

Always adding to his arsenal, Limbaugh has a knack for turning up political curiosities he can use. For instance, he came upon a 1962 speech by John Kennedy in which the president made a strong case for cutting tax rates. Limbaugh turned speech excerpts into an interview—"My conversation with John F. Kennedy"—and distributed it widely. JFK, says Limbaugh, would surely have been a dittohead.

More conventionally, he cites conservative economist Paul Craig Roberts, and data from the Commerce Department and Bureau of Labor Statistics to bolster his claims about substantial growth in manufacturing and job creation during the eighties. He uses plenty of other carefully selected figures to bolster his contention that "Reaganomics did work, and the gap between the rich and poor was narrowed rather than expanded" during Reagan's presidency.

John Kenneth Galbraith—certainly no Limbaugh ally—has noted that despite the attention accorded "the dismaying number of individuals and families that are very poor...the much larger number of Americans who live well above the poverty line and the very considerable number who live in comparative well-being have...occasioned much less comment." According to Galbraith, in 1989 12.8 percent of the population lived below the poverty line of $12,674 for a family of four, while 20 percent earned at least $50,000.[11]

Citing the wisdom of Texas Senator Phil Gramm, Limbaugh says: "Liberals like to achieve fairness by spreading the misery. Conservatives seek to expand opportunity." That's the kind of argument that seems to strike a resonant chord among Limbaugh's followers. It's the kind of argument that George Bush was unable to make convincingly in 1992.

"Expanded opportunity" means different things to different people. To the poor, it might mean a chance to get a job; to the rich, a rollback in capital gains taxes. However it is defined, it is a concept at the root of the American economic spirit. That is why it is such an effective part of the Limbaugh gospel.

His message seems to capture the essence of capitalism: "You should never apologize for trying to earn more money. Never feel guilty for wanting to keep more of it for you and your family. Do not accept the silly notion that there is poverty and suffering in America because you are greedy and aren't paying enough in taxes."

That is the kind of speech people—at least Limbaugh's people—like to hear. In its simplicity and conviction, it echoes Ronald Reagan. It's part politics and part preaching; part reality and part myth.

And it is quintessential Rush Limbaugh.

RUSH'S RADIO ANCESTORS

5

Eclipsed in recent years by television and considered by some to be the "forgotten medium," radio nevertheless retains its influence. Rush Limbaugh's clout is one manifestation of that.

Limbaugh is a creature of radio. To understand him, you must understand radio—its strengths, its limitations, and its history.

Limbaugh follows a long line of entertainers, journalists and political figures who have used radio to charm, inform, and cajole. From another era's quiet conversation of Arthur Godfrey and demagogic ranting of Huey Long, to the more recent poetic story telling of Garrison Keillor and reassuring homilies of Ronald Reagan, radio's history is filled with men and women who touched the listening public's hearts and minds.

A footnote from Ronald Reagan's career illustrates the political power of radio. In 1975, shortly after leaving the California governorship, Reagan was looking for ways to maintain his visibility and political options. He received two broadcasting offers: one from Mutual Radio to do a daily five-minute program, the other from CBS to alternate with Eric Sevareid as a commentator on the "CBS Evening News with Walter Cronkite." This was the nation's dominant newscast, and Reagan was to be given a twice-a-week slot.

Defying conventional wisdom, Reagan chose radio. He said radio has more credibility than television news, and when people listen to something rather than see it on TV, the message has more staying power. Long-time Reagan aide Michael Deaver says he is convinced Reagan was elected president because he was on the radio every day for five years and reached fifty million people each week.[1]

Radio was the medium of choice for Reagan—who understood the political psychology of the American people better than anyone else in recent years. It also is the keystone of the Limbaugh phenomenon. In building his career, Limbaugh has borrowed from the technique and ambition of his radio predecessors. He knows where he fits in the continuum of radio history.

A NEW WORLD

"What hath God wrought?" In addition to being a despairing liberal's question about Rush Limbaugh, that was the first official message sent on May 24, 1844, over Samuel F. B. Morse's new device, the telegraph. For the first time in history, people could communicate across great distances almost instantaneously, limited only by the need to string electric wire between points. By 1861, Americans could send messages from coast to coast.

Having the telegraph at their disposal, people were determined to use it. They sent their electric chatter zipping throughout the country. Content was not always as important as was transmitting for the sake of transmitting. "We are in great haste to construct a magnetic telegraph from Maine to Texas," said Henry David Thoreau, "but Maine and Texas, it may be, have nothing important to communicate. Either is in such a predicament as the man who was earnest to be introduced to a distinguished deaf woman, but when he was presented, and one end of her ear trumpet was put into his hand, had nothing to say. As if the main object were to talk fast and not to talk sensibly."[2]

Today, when life is permeated by telecommunications of various kinds, that issue of speed rather than sense remains very much with us.

As wondrous as the telegraph was, it allowed no truly personal conversation between individuals. The electronic messages were transmitted in code, so trained operators were needed to send and receive. Alexander Graham Bell responded to these problems when he filed a patent application in 1876 for his telephone.

The next step was to end dependence on wires. Radio did that, pushing aside many of the limitations of mass communication. Broadcasting might be as significant an innovation as movable type's replacement of hand copying was. Now, in addition to the point-to-point transmissions of telegraph and telephone, radio broadcasts could be made available to all who had the gear to receive them.

Amateur radio broadcasts began in America in 1906, and commercial broadcasting started in the 1920s, with networks operating by 1926.

Early on, politics found a place on the airwaves. Although some dispute exists about who put the first commercial broadcast on the air, the most commonly accepted source of the first scheduled, paid-for program is Pittsburgh's KDKA, which delivered election returns on November 2, 1920.

Consumers wanted to pluck this new product from the air. In 1924, Americans spent more than $350 million on radio sets. By 1927 more than five hundred AM stations had begun broadcasting.

Radio truly hit its stride during the Great Depression. People were looking for cheap entertainment; unable to afford going out, they stayed home and listened to the radio. Despite the nation's overall economic ill health, radio advertising revenues remained robust, climbing from $40 million in 1930 to $112 million in 1935 (while other mediums' advertising income was declining).[3]

Programming consisted largely of comedy, soap operas, action serials, and variety shows such as "Major Bowes and His Original Amateur Hour." Live music programs included jazz from the likes of Benny Goodman and Tommy Dorsey, and classical concerts conducted by Arturo Toscanini, first with the New York Philharmonic and later with NBC's own symphony orchestra.

Radio had rapidly become an integral part of American life. It was a principal source of entertainment and information, shaping public tastes and discourse.

Doing well on radio required certain skills. Stage talent didn't always lead to effective radio performance. Radio "personalities" played to millions of fans who could hear but not see them. That meant communicating an invisible, but winning presence across the air waves and into the audience's living rooms.

A 1935 survey found that 65 percent of radio listeners preferred comedy above other programs. Vaudeville stars such as Fred Allen, Jack Benny, Jimmy Durante, and Eddie Cantor made the transition to radio based on a good understanding of what routines worked without visual support. Performers who relied heavily on sight gags obviously would have trouble. Many of those who didn't adjust to radio's demands found their careers fading away as vaudeville declined.

The successful radio comedians learned to mix their written material with other aural assets. Sound effects or music might be added. Or sometimes mere silence was used. For example, Jack Benny's "H'mm" and pregnant pauses between set-up and punch line were a product of his impeccable timing. They worked on the stage, in his films, later on television, and on radio, too.

But the pauses had to be part of the rhythm of the material, because they had no support from gestures or other visual aid. One review of a comedian's sketch noted that the performer was successful because she refrained from "pausing after each wisecrack for a laugh. Nobody laughs out loud at a radio joke anyway, so such pauses are simply flat."[4]

Silence on the stage could be accompanied by movement or facial expression to which the audience could respond in much the same way as they would react to words. Silence on radio works differently. It provides space for the listener's imagination to operate—for thinking about what has just been heard and anticipating what will come next. Limbaugh, for instance, often uses pauses to underscore a point he has just made. He gives listeners time to mull over his wisdom or others' folly and to say to themselves, "You're right, Rush."

As radio techniques were developing, performers had to adjust their styles. Consider the difficulty faced by entertainers who had spent their entire careers playing before live audiences—getting immediate, steady feedback—and then switching to radio. They would toss their material out into the ether and hope that somewhere out there people were laughing or crying or humming or doing whatever it was the entertainer wanted them to do.

Doing radio requires solid self-confidence. Some radio programs were produced in front of studio audiences not only to add the vitality of applause and laughter to the performance reaching the home audience, but also to keep the entertainers from feeling so isolated.

Connections between the early radio comics and Limbaugh are not always visible, but they exist, linking him to radio's traditions. Limbaugh has said that he will be successful only as long as he entertains, and that his goal is to win and hold audiences. That means he must employ the tricks of his trade and use radio to its greatest advantage.

He likes this medium: "I look at radio as just the stage on which I perform best. It is there that I can be myself. I don't have to get make-up, I don't have to listen to fifteen producers and directors lining up a camera shot. I'm a totally spontaneous person. TV is not spontaneous."[5]

While being spontaneous, Limbaugh relies on some aural gimmicks. He snaps the paper he is reading (often one of the thousands of news items faxed to him by fans around the country). After he has read and commented about the material, his listeners hear him loudly crumpling the paper—particularly if its contents have displeased him. He punctuates his comments by knocking on his desk and precedes his "news updates" with a trumpet-less fanfare: "Dadalup, dadalup, dadalup!"

He also cues in various sound effects: "When Johnny Comes Marching Home" while mentioning Ross Perot; chain saws when chastising "environmental wackos"; the strains of "Born Free" competing with gunfire when zinging "animal rights wackos"; and, most controversially, the whoosh of a vacuum cleaner mixed with a scream while performing "caller abortions" on calls he didn't like.

This last stunt brought accusations, Limbaugh later said, of "insensitivity, cruelty, meanness, and a lack of decency." He canceled caller abortions after two weeks, but defended them as a legitimate reflection of his antiabortion stance.

He said on the air: "To the extent that I may have heightened awareness out there, I believe I have done a service, regardless of how distasteful it may have been to some....If you didn't know in your heart of hearts that abortion was a savage, violent act, what I did wouldn't have bugged you so much. I took you inside an abortion mill, and some of you couldn't take it. You can't handle it when it was only dramatized. Yet, you're not bothered by abortion when it happens for real. Is there not a contradiction here? Think about it."

Usually, Limbaugh lets his words stand alone. But he understands radio's strengths and knows how to use them to add more punch to his arguments. With a few seconds of sound effects, he adds a dimension of drama and—as his listeners' reactions to "caller abortions" indicated—of power to his pronouncements about this issue.

He also knows that many in his audience take the matters he discusses even more seriously than he does. The reaction to his treatment of the abortion issue—which he says "threatens to become this nation's next civil war"—reflects this. (He says that after his on-air explanation of his purpose very few people called to argue with him.)

But dealing with such issues shouldn't be done without recognizing that a difference exists between temperate, thoughtful discourse, and incendiary provocation. Limbaugh usually responds gently when he senses a caller is truly upset. He judges the mood and temperament of callers and usually does not bait those who disagree with him. He normally refrains from the semantic games in which an experienced radio talker will always prevail over a nervous caller. When he engages, however, in what he considers to be playful verbal jabbing, his playfulness often includes further references to "wackos" and "Commie libs" and such. This tends to raise further the blood pressure of callers who don't share his sense of humor.

But he's not unredeemably bullheaded. He sometimes responds to being told that he doesn't know enough about a topic by expressing willingness to get more information.

In his "caller abortions" and other use of manipulative drama—minimalist as it may be—he is working with a broadcast technique that dates back to radio's early days. Limbaugh's sallies sometimes are tasteless, but he often brings to radio a mix of childish mischief and professional zeal like that which characterized Orson Welles's memorable production of "War of the Worlds" in 1938. Then, Welles and his Mercury Theater colleagues were astonished by the hurricane force of a mere radio show. But the hysteria their invasion from Mars stimulated was early proof that the medium's influence should not be underrated.

TALK RADIO AS A COMPANION

Gentler traditions also helped shape the radio world in which Limbaugh thrives. His skill of talking *with* rather than talking *at* an audience is a hallmark he shares with Arthur Godfrey, who understood that radio is as much a companion to people as it is a mechanical dispenser of programming.

In a radio career that stretched from 1929 to 1972, Godfrey gave the impression of sitting across from you at the kitchen table, just chatting; he was like a member of the family.

His show's hallmark was its spontaneity. He would eat breakfast between musical numbers, talk about products that weren't even his sponsors while teasing the companies that *were* his sponsors, abandon his script, ask the orchestra to play unrehearsed songs, and otherwise keep cast and audience on their toes. All this worked. At one point in his career, CBS estimated he was reaching forty million people each week.[6]

When Godfrey burst into tears while covering the funeral of Franklin Roosevelt for CBS, his sadness was felt across the nation by those for whom he was much more than just a voice coming over the air. He was kin.

Such rapport is the goal of every broadcaster. Even on television, merely being seen does not ensure that a network anchorperson or other luminary will be perceived as a "real person." Some TV coaches urge their students to "make love to the camera" to be certain their charm will ooze into viewers' living rooms. Anatomical grotesqueries aside, the usual product of such amorousness is likely to be merely a toothy apparition radiating pre-fab emotions from the screen. For every viewer-friendly Charles Kuralt, there are dozens of earnest men and women who remain forever remote as slightly out-of-focus "TV personalities."

Limbaugh—even in the midst of one of his many long soliloquies—is more a talker-with than talker-at. He is trying to convince *you*—his sole listener.

His free-flowing, ad-lib style works well, rolling across the bumps and dips of conversation.

Even the mock ponderousness he often employs is clearly a put-on. His tone and content are geared to middle America.

You turn on the radio and there's your pal Rush. Pull up a stool, have a beer, and let's talk about what's wrong with those idiots in Washington.

That's how Limbaugh uses radio. It gives him power; he gives it power.

STORY TELLING

Another contemporary radio master is Garrison Keillor. In the content of their work, he and Limbaugh couldn't be more different. Instead of Limbaugh's forceful polemics, Keillor offers gentle story telling.

Like Limbaugh, Keillor became intrigued by radio at an early age. "As a child," he says, "I stood in the closet and pretended I was on the radio, talking into the handle of my mother's Hoover upright vacuum." He cares little for television, and remains devoted to radio: "There's no romance in television; it's just the Wal-Mart of the mind. Radio is infinitely sexier."[7]

And like Ronald Reagan, Keillor has regard for the lasting impact that can be made through radio. "The spoken word, not pictures, is the doorway to memory. The simple, depressing fact about going on television is that nobody remembers ten minutes later a single thing you said. If I tell stories on radio, I will run into people months and years later who can repeat back to me what I said, word for word. This never ceases to amaze."[8]

In subtle ways, Keillor's and Limbaugh's popularity shares some common ground. Tales about Lake Wobegon, Keillor's fictive home, evoke a longing among many listeners for simpler, small-town America. This is the same effect advertising executive Hal Riney aimed for with his "It's morning again" television spots for the 1984 Reagan campaign. This also is the America Limbaugh implicitly harkens back to when he touts conservative values. Nostalgia can override realism; pictures of the past— softened into pleasing fuzziness by the passage of time—are easier to look upon than are harshly realistic depictions of the present.

A TRUSTED MEDIUM

Limbaugh also owes some of his credibility to those who made radio a trusted medium for news. The most influential and thoughtful of these was Edward R. Murrow.

Particularly during the years immediately preceding U.S. entry into World War II, Murrow was relied upon by millions of Americans to tell them what was really going on. From 1939 to 1941, when Great Britain stood largely alone and many American politicians remained enraptured by iso-lationist fantasies, Murrow gave interventionists an invaluable boost with his sympathetic portraits of Britons under fire.

Here is an excerpt of a broadcast from London during the Nazi blitz: "This is London. And the raid which started about seven hours ago is still in progress....Once tonight an antiaircraft battery opened fire just as I drove past. It lifted me from the seat and a hot wind swept over the car....And so London is waiting for dawn. We ought to get the all clear in about another two hours. Then those big German bombers that have been lumbering and mumbling about overhead all night will have to go home."[9]

He watched his medium become ever more powerful, sometimes with questionable effect. In a 1937 speech, Murrow noted, "New and more powerful stations are being erected in order that nation may hurl invective at nation....Radio crosses boundaries and fortunately or unfortunately there is no one there to inspect the contents of its luggage."[10]

In the same speech he addressed the broadcaster's duties. Radio, he said, "has enormous power...but it has no character, no conscience of its own. It reflects the hatreds, the jealousies and ambitions of those men and governments that control it." And on another occasion, Murrow wrote, "Radio in a democracy must be more than an industry, more than a medium of entertainment, more than a source of revenue for those who own the facilities."[11]

At least in his writings and public pronouncements, Limbaugh has been slow to acknowledge this need to match power with responsibility. His critics argue that his one-sidedness when he discusses issues amounts to abuse of this power, or at least a failure to respect the influence of a medium that assumes the character of those who use it.

Murrow, like his colleagues on the entertainment side of radio, understood how the rules of rhetoric had to be changed to make broadcasting effective. He wrote: "The only recipe for making a speaker understand the demands and limitations of radio as a medium is to ask him to imagine himself standing before his own fireplace, perhaps leaning with one elbow on the mantel, talking to six or eight people in his own home. His visitors might include a business associate, a university professor, a couple of day laborers....The speaker, as the host, must engage the interest of all....He will engage the interest of millions if he can discover the essential intimacy of a medium which puts every listener within whispering distance of his lips."[12]

Murrow was still serving his apprenticeship at CBS when he wrote that appraisal, but it was a practical guideline that he followed throughout his career.

Intimacy enhances intensity. Limbaugh— who tries to remove barriers between his listeners and himself—apparently knows that.

STAYING POWER
Murrow and many of his younger radio colleagues (such as Walter Cronkite and Howard K. Smith) moved into television during the 1950s and built that medium's journalism. But radio has by no means been forsaken. Among the most popular broadcasts—radio or TV—in the country is Paul Harvey's daily smorgasbord of human interest news items. With an annual salary of roughly $10 million and a network of more than twelve

hundred ABC affiliates, Harvey—even more than Limbaugh—has proved that radio has staying power.

Radio has advantages over television, among which are its portability and its role as provider of background words and music. People carry little transistor radios or mammoth boom boxes wherever they go, to listen to baseball games or rock or news. Drivers rely on their car radios for respite from the agonies of traffic jams. You can watch the road and listen to a radio, and despite the increasing proliferation of tiny TVs, you cannot drive while watching television. "Drive time"—which for many unfortunates is several hours every workday—ensures continuing economic sustenance for radio as advertisers delightedly use the airwaves to reach these gridlocked consumers.

As competition between radio and television grew, radio tried to carve a niche separate from that which television had occupied. Stations emphasized specialized formats (rock, country, ethnic, news-talk, and others) and programming geared to local interests. While much of the television day was given over to the national network schedule, many radio stations were able to target the wants and needs of their hometown audience. (With the growing proliferation of local cable television stations, this part of the radio-TV battle is likely to take on a new ferocity.)

These factors have helped radio escape the doom that was predicted for it while television's early popularity soared. Some statistics are instructive: In 1992, Americans bought seventy-one million radios at a cost of $2.6 billion. The number of radios in the country has increased 20 percent since 1980. Average daily listening time is more than three hours, and 77 percent of Americans listen to radio every day, 96 percent at least once a week.[13]

Nevertheless, the economic picture for many radio enterprises is not bright. In the intense competition spawned by deregulation, more than half the nation's commercial stations were operating at a loss in 1992.[14] That makes a solid audience-grabber like Limbaugh an even greater prize.

Besides the approximately ninety-seven hundred commercial stations, listeners can choose from among roughly sixteen hundred noncommercial outlets. Here is where fans of classical music, jazz, public affairs discussions, and a variety of unconventional formats can find the programming that profit-hungry commercial broadcasters think is too esoteric.

Dominating this field is National Public Radio. Born in 1970, it is backed by money from the Corporation for Public Broadcasting, foundations, businesses, and individual donors. NPR has proved that dependence on public funding and high quality programming are perfectly compatible.

With shows such as "All Things Considered," "Morning Edition," and "Marketplace," NPR has set and met high standards. Its news programming is sophisticated but not obscure and weathers periodic charges that it is too liberal. NPR news has fostered similarly ambitious efforts from many local public stations.

NPR's reporting about national issues often puts commercial broadcast organizations to shame. Recognizing that the public's business is usually too complicated to be suited to sound-bite summaries, NPR offers time and thoughtfulness missing from much other news coverage.

SHOCK RADIO

Far removed from public radio's offerings is the barrage of coarseness served up by exponents of "shock" or "blue" radio. This kind of programming should remove any doubts about the depths to which public taste can sink. Its most successful practitioner is Howard Stern, a specialist in sexual and scatological humor that apparently has considerable appeal—at least enough to ensure a seven-digit income for Stern. In some markets, local disc jockeys emulating Stern offer their own versions of racist and sexist cleverness.

The Federal Communications Commission has declared itself appalled and imposed some fines, most notably on Stern, who seems unfazed by officialdom's unhappiness. (In 1992, the FCC fined Stern's employer, Infinity Broadcasting Company, $600,000 for indecent broadcasts by Stern. The FCC also fined a Los Angeles station $105,000 for carrying these broadcasts.) Market forces, not the FCC, probably will do the most to determine the longevity of this genre.

Among talk show hosts, Stern and Limbaugh garner by far the highest ratings. They have little else in common. Limbaugh usually ignores Stern. Stern refers to Limbaugh as a "fat pig."

AIRWAVE POLITICIANS

Although Limbaugh can claim as radio ancestors an impressive roster of entertainers and journalists, he may be more closely related to political figures who used radio to spread their messages and recruit followers.

Among the first of these was Father Charles Coughlin, a Catholic priest who began broadcasting in 1926 from the Shrine of the Little Flower in Royal Oak, Michigan, a suburb of Detroit. As the country sank into the Great Depression, Coughlin blasted President Herbert Hoover and the "banksters" who were ruining the "common people." Known as the "radio priest," he was noted for the sense of urgency with which he infused his messages. One writer observed, "He manages always to speak as though his words of warning were being uttered just two jumps ahead of the crack of doom."[15]

Also, Coughlin possessed "extraordinary skills as a performer," using the "warm, inviting sound of his voice, a sound that could make even the tritest statements sound richer and more meaningful than they actually were."[16]

For a while, Coughlin was a strong supporter of Franklin Roosevelt. He first told his listeners, "The New Deal is Christ's Deal," but later announced that Roosevelt was in league with the "godless capitalists, the Jews, communists, international bankers, and plutocrats."[17]

Swinging back and forth across the ideological spectrum, Coughlin said, "In politics I am neither Republican, Democrat, nor Socialist. I glory in the fact that I am a simple Catholic priest endeavoring to inject Christianity into the fabric of an economic system woven upon the loom of greed by the cunning fingers of those who manipulate the shuttles of human lives for their own selfish purposes."[18]

Coughlin didn't rely on subtlety. He attacked those he judged to be on the wrong side of issues as "fanatics," "scoundrels," and "lying voices."[19] He became too controversial for CBS and so set up his own network, which by 1935 included thirty-one stations, at that time a substantial number, with considerable reach throughout the country.

He mixed a deluge of economic statistics (often of mysterious origin) with invocations of Christianity. He seemed to have a sense of how to appeal to Middle America. In his heyday, Coughlin had a fervid following. He received an average of eighty thousand pieces of mail each week. After one denunciation of "Hoover prosperity," a million letters poured in. His criticism of the World Court produced two hundred thousand telegrams to the U.S. Senate. For followers who couldn't get enough of him, he started a magazine, *Social Justice* (which never became as influential as his broadcasts were).

Eventually, Coughlin's anti-Semitism and increasing shrillness began scaring away stations. By 1940, he was in marked decline.

EVERY MAN A KING

Another strident voice of opposition to Roosevelt was that of Louisiana Senator Huey Long. One of FDR's allies said that Coughlin and other critics "were all pygmies compared with Huey."[20] Trumpeting his slogan, "Every man a king, but no one wears a crown," Long proposed a "Share Our Wealth" plan based on high taxes, confiscation and redistribution.

Roosevelt's top political advisor, James A. Farley, said Long's speaking was "a curious hodge-podge of buffoonery and demagogic strutting, cleverly bundled in with a lot of shrewd common sense and an evangelical fervor...." The Louisianan's analysis of economic problems was unfailingly simplistic—he admitted he wasn't sure exactly how "Share Our Wealth" would be implemented—but his wildly folksy appeals to the hopes and fears of the working class won him a huge following.

Long claimed to have inspired formation of twenty-seven thousand Share Our Wealth clubs with more than seven million members. Farley and other Democratic strategists saw him as potentially a major threat to Roosevelt's reelection chances in 1936, especially if Long and Coughlin formed an alliance. A secret Democratic Party poll indicated that Long might win four million votes if he ran as third-party candidate.[21]

Radio speeches were an important part of Long's long-range plan to build a national base. He featured a studied folksiness and careful vagueness about implementing his policies, but his smooth on-air delivery rivaled Roosevelt's. He gave six nationally broadcast speeches during the first three months of 1935, and on average received more than one hundred thousand letters after each one.

Speculation about Long's presidential prospects ended in September 1935, when he was shot and killed in a hallway of the Louisiana capitol in Baton Rouge.

COMPARISONS

As they played on the public's emotions, Coughlin and Long could be venomous and manipulative. They used radio to fuel class and ethnic hatreds. In almost every way, they operated far differently than Limbaugh ever has.

But some comparisons are instructive. Coughlin was not seeking office. As just the "simple Catholic priest" he claimed to be, he retained a political credibility that run-of-the-mill politicians could not sustain. He relied on his "outsider" status to enhance his influence. Limbaugh does much the same.

Long had become a powerful force in Louisiana through political hustle and intimidation well before he began taking advantage of radio. As a senator, could carry an "outsider" claim only so far. But he did establish himself—although a Democrat— as the dominant voice of an otherwise inchoate opposition to Roosevelt and the New Deal. Long used radio speeches to build his national identity.

He had a golden opportunity. The Republicans were in such disarray that they could deliver few coherent opposition positions to the public. They had held the White House for the past twelve years until a relatively young governor evicted them. Sound familiar?

The political dynamics of the 1990s are far less volatile than were those of the 1930s, but in both cases a vacuum awaited filling by an unconventional figure. In September 1993, the leading conservative magazine, *National Review*, presented its readers with an idealized portrait of

Limbaugh on its cover and a story titled, "The Leader of the Opposition." As much question as statement, this headline apparently evolved from the presumption that Bob Dole, Phil Gramm, Jack Kemp, and other Republican luminaries were not sufficiently inspiring to merit being made commander of the anti-Clinton forces.

Limbaugh, however, not only has a massive and still-growing following, but also clearly understands what it means to be in opposition. Even while touting Bush's candidacy in 1992, he knew that he would be livelier and more controversial as Clinton critic than as Bush booster.

Long is said by some to have forced Roosevelt to move to the left as a preemptive measure. Limbaugh probably would be delighted if his hectoring could push Clinton the other way.

WILL'S WIT AND WISDOM

One radio-using contemporary of Long and Coughlin was more popular than either of them, and was their polar opposite in tone: Will Rogers.

Jack Kemp has compared Limbaugh to Rogers, saying that Limbaugh's verbal war against the Clinton administration has been waged "with wit, wisdom, humor, tenacity, and an irrepressible style."[22]

Although he talked a lot about politics—usually displaying great insight—Rogers had clearly defined his role. He was an entertainer.

Although he was more influential than most politicians, he was not trying to become a political power and had no interest in wading into partisan battles. He said, "It's getting so if a man wants to stand well socially, he can't afford to be seen with either the Democrats or the Republicans."

But Rogers was in fact willing to be seen with both. During his long career, he was friendly with presidents of both parties: Republicans Theodore Roosevelt, Calvin Coolidge, and Herbert Hoover; Democrats Woodrow Wilson and Franklin Roosevelt. The only chief executive with whom he didn't hit it off was Warren Harding.

In 1933, Rogers began a series of Sunday-night radio broadcasts. After a few musical numbers, Rogers offered a fifteen-minute monologue based primarily on the week's news. Everything was fair game: Democrats, Republicans, repeal of Prohibition—even Mahatma Gandhi. A veteran stage performer, Rogers had some trouble adapting to radio, calling it "the toughest test a comedian has." He insisted on having a studio audience for his show, and brought an alarm clock on stage with him so he wouldn't run past his allotted time.[23]

Limbaugh would certainly agree with some of Rogers's observations, such as, "We are a nation that runs in spite of, and not on account of, our government," and, "You get more for not working than you will for working, and more for not raising a hog than raising it."

But it is hard to imagine Limbaugh treating Bill Clinton as gently as Rogers referred to Hoover's responsibility for the Depression: "Don't you go and blame the Republicans for everything that's happened to us. They're not smart enough to have thought it up."

Limbaugh, like virtually every other commentator who uses topical humor, owes something to Rogers. But Kemp's comparison doesn't work when Limbaugh's frequent partisanship and stridency are considered. Rogers and Limbaugh may be professionally related, but they are distant cousins.

FIRESIDE ROOSEVELT

While Will Rogers's broadcasts were helping Americans laugh through hard times, Franklin Roosevelt was using radio with unprecedented expertise to consolidate his political authority.

Roosevelt's prowess became obvious during the 1932 presidential campaign. Incumbent Herbert Hoover's on-air performance was described as "an old-fashioned phonograph in need of winding," but professional broadcasters were impressed by FDR's "ability to create a feeling of intimacy between himself and his listeners, and his adroitness in presenting complicated matters in such simple terms that the man in the street believes he has full mastery of them."[24]

As president, Roosevelt recognized what an asset radio could be. He rallied public support through his "fireside chats" and many other radio addresses. The New Deal was further bolstered by the radio speeches of Eleanor Roosevelt, cabinet members, and other officials.

Roosevelt's main contribution to the radio history of which Limbaugh is a part was his elevating the medium from a supplemental to principal political tool. Just as Roosevelt relied on radio to deliver his message, so too did the public increasingly count on this medium to showcase politicians and their programs and otherwise to provide news. A 1940 poll found that 52 percent of Americans used radio as their main source of political information, compared to 38 percent who depended mainly on newspapers.[25]

Today, Bill Clinton uses weekly radio broadcasts to present his version of what he is trying to accomplish. He can do this more frequently and with greater control on radio than on television, where unedited air time is harder to come by.

Limbaugh also knows that Americans are accustomed to getting political information from the radio. He counts on the frequency and pervasiveness of his message to make him competitive with the president as broadcaster. In politics, radio is a great equalizer.

LIKE REAGAN, LIKE LIMBAUGH

A much closer broadcasting and political kinship exists between Limbaugh and Ronald Reagan. Like Limbaugh, Reagan began his career as a small-town broadcaster. He began at station WOC, which described itself in its sign-off as, "owned and operated by the Palmer School of Chiropractic, the Chiropractic Fountainhead, Davenport, Iowa, where the West begins and in the state where the tall corn grows..."[26]

Also like Limbaugh, Reagan managed to get fired early in his career, but he was almost immediately rehired and before long made a name for himself as a sportscaster. His particular skill was taking terse telegraphic copy of a baseball game in progress and embellish it so he sounded as if he were actually at the game.

Reagan soon moved from Iowa broadcasting into California movie making. But he would return to radio, using it to help sustain his political career.

The merging of sportscasting and political broadcasting skills was not difficult for Reagan. He had learned in Iowa how to hold an audience, using much the same technique that Ed Murrow and other skilled radio stars had mastered.

As he recounts in his autobiography, Reagan had friends who would gather in a local barber shop to listen to his renditions of baseball games. "I began to picture these friends down at the shop when I was on the air and, knowing they were there, I'd try to imagine how my words sounded to them and how they were reacting, and I'd adjust accordingly and spoke as if I was speaking personally to them. There was a specific audience out there I could see in my mind, and I sort of aimed my words at them....I started getting mail from people all over the Midwest who told me I sounded as if I was talking directly and personally to *them*. Over the years, I've always remembered that. I try to remember that audiences are made up of individuals and I try to speak as if I am talking to a group of friends...not to millions, but to a handful of people in a living room...or a barbershop."[27]

After completing his second term as governor of California, Reagan was preparing to run for president, but needed to bide his time while post-Watergate turmoil quieted. (He had already made one brief, unsuccessful foray as a presidential candidate, mounting a minor challenge to Richard Nixon in 1968.) The politically safest—and certainly the most lucrative—way to do that was to merchandise himself and his ideas through the media. Within months after leaving office, his radio commentaries were being carried by more than two hundred stations, his column appeared in 174 newspapers, and he was making up to ten speeches a month for $5,000 each. His income as governor had been $49,100; the following year his politics-as-business ventures had raised it to approximately $800,000.[28]

The approach and at least short-range goals of Reagan and Limbaugh are strikingly similar: Use a multimedia strategy to define yourself as a conservative champion, and—not incidentally—to make lots of money.

Reagan's five-minute radio commentaries were characterized by their optimism and conservatism. His points often relied wholly on anecdotal evidence, but he possessed the expert salesman's ability to sound unfailingly convincing. These spots gave him a forum to discuss national issues, to demonstrate especially to those familiar with him only as an actor that he was not a political freak.

He delivered his messages silkily enough and made many of his points temperately enough to glide over fears that his philosophy was warmed-over Goldwater-like extremism. The political value of Reagan's broadcasts was found in the consistent presence they let him establish, rather than in their specific content. Especially for diehard conservatives looking for someone to lead them into the White House, Reagan's electronic eloquence was convincing evidence that he should carry the conservative banner.

Although unsuccessful in his effort to wrest the 1976 nomination away from the appointed incumbent, Gerald Ford, Reagan positioned himself as dominant candidate in the run-up to the 1980 race.

As candidate Reagan's rise continued, radio's importance to him lessened. Television and a full-blown campaign apparatus began conveying his image and message to the public. But even after he had won the White House, Reagan found radio helpful as a supplement to other modes of maintaining visibility and making his case. He delivered weekly radio speeches about topics of the moment, a practice continued by Presidents Bush and Clinton.

Along with his ideological affinity for Reagan, Limbaugh shares with the former president an understanding of how to hold an audience while delivering even a prosaic political message. Although Limbaugh's style is often more grating than is Reagan's, Limbaugh has cast himself as a more aggressive advocate. Reagan was the general, Limbaugh the commando.

RADIO LEGACIES

Rush Limbaugh's success is due partly to his politics, but also largely to his skill in merging the talents of his media ancestors. For instance, "intimacy" is cited as an important element of the work of radio users such as Edward R. Murrow, Franklin Roosevelt, and many entertainers. Limbaugh, too, knows it is an intrinsic part of radio's influence. The warm intensity of callers to his show reflects his success at building intimate links to his audience.

Another factor often mentioned as a characteristic of the radio work of politicians such as

Roosevelt and Reagan, and performers such as Will Rogers is the ability to speak about issues in ways that the general public can understand. Roosevelt, for example, won backing for his New Deal reforms in part because he could convince average Americans that they had a vested interest in his legislative program. Limbaugh is not afraid to address complex topics, but he is remarkably skillful at making his listeners understand—or at least think they understand—what he is talking about.

Critics argue that this success is due to one-sidedness, that Limbaugh sacrifices fairness in order to make his case convincing. Further, the critics contend, since he prefers edicts to debates, these simplistic versions of issues go unchallenged except by the occasional caller who is not a dedicated dittohead.

Limbaugh's absolutism certainly might produce lopsided support for the gospel according to Rush. But perhaps that underestimates at least part of the public. Judging by an unscientifically random sampling of his callers' comments, most—including those who agree with him—are not mindlessly following him. They are thinking; some are stimulated enough to seek information from additional sources. This is not evidence that an army of political zombies is taking shape.

So Limbaugh marches on, to whatever tune he chooses. Although not all his radio ancestors would be happy to claim him as a descendant, and even though he is branching out into more nonradio endeavors, he clearly remains a creation of this medium.

Limbaugh says he expects to have his "own wing in the Radio Hall of Fame." It's too early to tell whether he'll get it, but the architects might want to prepare some blueprints.

YOU'RE ON THE AIR

6

In some ways, Rush Limbaugh's success is due to his being in the right place at the right time.

Besides filling a gap in conservative political ranks, he has emerged as a major star of a broadcast genre that happened to surge in popularity just as his national show was getting underway. This is not to detract from Limbaugh's gifts as entertainer and polemicist, but his timing could not have been better even if it had been carefully planned.

For advertisers, politicians, and others who pay close attention to trends and fads in the mass media, talk radio looks to be the big story of the 1990s. The king of this domain is now Limbaugh, but plenty of ambitious princes are also in the business.

Talk radio's history antedates Limbaugh, and the factors that make the genre so popular have existed even longer than that. Talk programming is rooted in the public's thirst for diverse kinds of information. Standard news, weather, sports, stock market reports, and the like are only partly satisfying. Some people want to hear religious programs or Hollywood gossip. Others want tips about cooking or car repairs. Many like discussions of current issues. And some just enjoy hearing other voices talking about anything.

Whether the radio is offering information, entertainment, or company (or some combination of these), it is delivering the outside world into its audience's living rooms. Radio careers rise or fall based on the ability to provide whatever the public currently wants to have coming over the airwaves and into their homes.

Talk radio got its start in the 1920s with religious programs such as "National Vespers" and the "Catholic Hour." Occasionally, sermons became political, as was the case with Father Charles Coughlin.

Household hints also were in demand, so in 1928 the U.S. Department of Agriculture helped produce the "National Farm and Home Hour."

Predecessors of Limbaugh-like, issues-oriented programming also appeared during radio's early years. In 1933, NBC began carrying "The University of Chicago Roundtable," a panel of faculty and occasional guests discussing current affairs. That might sound like a heavy program, but it remained on the air for twenty-five years. Along the same lines, NBC in 1935 began offering "America's Town Meeting of the Air," during which studio audience members could offer their opinions about the topic of the day.

The Limbaugh-like host also began appearing on the scene. Walter Winchell, his appeal based on his brash toughness, began his gossip show on NBC in 1932. Winchell's popularity helped the talk format evolve during the 1940s. Program hosts stationed themselves at fancy New York restaurants and saloons, interviewing celebrities who dropped by.

Listener call-in shows began in the 1930s, but the callers weren't heard on the air; the host paraphrased their comments. During the 1950s, local talk shows started putting callers on the air, sometimes relying on tape delay mechanisms to avoid obscene surprises.

A major transformation of the talk show business came with the deregulation of the telephone industry in the 1980s. The ensuing competition drove down long-distance rates and made 800-numbers commonplace. At about the same time, satellite technology was making it much less expensive for networks to feed programming to affiliates. (Previously that had required costly use of telephone lines.)

These factors combined to make the national talk show practical. Without this new technology, Limbaugh might still be only a local star, dealing with caller complaints about potholes and trash pick-ups rather than the more cosmic issues he prefers.

Also, despite the conventional wisdom that declares radio to be a local medium, *talk* radio might be well-suited for a national audience. Topics are less site-specific, but listeners everywhere have opinions about national issues. And local talk shows are expensive, requiring extra staff and equipment. So, picking up a national program—even if that means paying a fee and a share of advertising revenue—might be less costly.

In many markets, talk radio was originally consigned to late-night time slots and the programs were seen as magnets for nutty callers with chips on their shoulders. The conventional wisdom said that the audience might be intense and loyal, but would never grow past a certain point.

Proponents of that thesis failed to take into account one of the mainstays of Limbaugh's popularity: Talk radio can be entertaining. The host need not be just a passive receiver of frequently inarticulate (and sometimes incoherent) calls, but rather can set the pace, debate, joke, and otherwise provide a stylistic signature to the program.

Limbaugh has cited passion and empathy as crucial elements in the making of a good talk show host. "Passion is the absolute best ingredient in what any communicator has, whether it's the caller or the host. If there's no passion, there's nothing. Here's where empathy is key. The most required characteristic of a good broadcaster is empathy with the listener; he has to know when the listener is going to tune out—and then do it first."[1]

Sometimes this produced some odd shows. For example, during the early 1970s, a Los Angeles station featured "Feminine Forum," which attracted callers such as the woman who took her son-in-law to bed to teach him better sexual technique...for her daughter's benefit, of course. Dubbed "topless radio," this kind of program elicited criticism from FCC chairman Dean Burch, who in 1973 said it was a "new breed of air pollution....with the suggestive, coaxing, pear-shaped tones of the smut-hustling host." This and other early forerunners of Howard Stern's show faded quickly in the face of such denunciations, especially when the FCC backed up its displeasure with fines.[2]

Another controversial program was hosted by Joe Pyne, who has been referred to as a "Cro-Magnon Rush Limbaugh." Pyne was ultraconservative, but unlike Limbaugh his specialty was to insult his callers and try his best to humiliate them.

These quirky programs found an audience, at least for a while. But they were insecure in their niches because the narrowness of their appeal made them highly vulnerable to even minor shifts in public mood and taste. Limbaugh seems to have learned some lessons from this. He never creates a vicious host-versus-caller dynamic such as Pyne featured, and he is careful not to let his monologues or discussions with callers to slip beyond the bounds of mainstream tastefulness.

Overall, talk radio continues to meet the interests of diverse audiences. National and local programs include the likes of Limbaugh's conservatism and Stern's smarminess, with plenty of other kinds of talk offerings. This breadth of format has contributed to a remarkable rise in talk radio's popularity.

According to a report in *Broadcasting* magazine, the number of stations using talk format more than tripled recently, rising from 238 in 1987 to 875 in 1992. Another approximately five hundred stations offer some talk programming each day. Also, the ratings share won by talk programs increased by 14 percent between early 1991 and 1992.[3]

The popularity of this format is not limited to the United States. For example, in 1993, even Beijing People's Radio offered a late-night phone-in show hosted by Pamela Pak Wan Kam, who had become famous for her flamboyant Hong Kong-based program. Although her audience had grown to fifteen million in just six weeks, Chinese officials took the program off the air, deciding that what might be acceptable in Hong Kong would not do in a nation that views liberalization warily.

Pak says, "People find it nice to have someone to talk to, someone to listen to and analyze and bring out new thinking." New thinking, however, is not always popular. She advised abused wives to leave their husbands, counseled husbands about relationships with their mistresses, and openly discussed homosexuality. Calls included complaints about financial problems and stress produced by China's economic growing pains. Even prison inmates managed to call, some of whom had been locked up for their role in the 1989 Tianamen Square protests.

All this was too much for Chinese officials, who decided that Pak should stay in Hong Kong and use prerecorded questions and answers, which then would be flown to Beijing for editing and broadcast. Pak turned down that proposal, saying, "I will wait for a chance to come back."[4]

Pamela Pak Wan Kam and her American counterparts share important common ground: Millions of people want to listen to them, and advertisers hunger to reach these large audiences. Sponsors such as Swatch watches and Elizabeth Arden cosmetics bought spots on Pak's show, eager to tap into one of the world's largest markets. Similarly, U.S. advertisers put their money where the ratings are—programs such as Limbaugh's.

A DEMOCRATIC DIALOGUE

"I used to vote only once a year, but now I vote early and often—with my mouth. Whenever there's something on the nation's mind, I turn on the radio, tune in the conversation of democracy and call up to get my own two cents' worth in."[5]

Those are observations of a *Smithsonian* magazine essayist. "The conversation of democracy" is a good description of the dialogue that is the essence of talk radio. Limbaugh—more than many talk hosts—dominates this dialogue, often turning it into monologue—his.

He frequently has said, "This show is not about what callers think, but what I think." That comment reinforces Limbaugh's largely self-created image as master of braggadocio. But his listeners get much more than Limbaugh as Limbaugh. They hear views that are often hard to find in what Limbaugh calls "the dominant media," and they hear callers who are often well-informed or at least highly interested in their topics, and who engage Limbaugh in thought-provoking discussion.

That, after all, is what Limbaugh's program is about. It is not—and does not pretend to be—a newscast. He differentiates between his view of "the way things ought to be" and what he recognizes to be the way things are. Above all, he wants to keep his show entertaining.

Limbaugh's success—his being in the right place at the right time—is only in part a function of format. Behind the popularity of talk radio is frustration that has given rise to an electronic activism. Rather than taking to the streets, dissatisfied Americans are taking to the airwaves.

To some extent, Limbaugh's "take-on-the-government" style—more than his precise political philosophy—matches the public mood. People are skeptical about the intentions and competence of "the establishment" in its many forms, and Lim-baugh—despite his fairly conventional Republicanism—is seen as an anti-establishment champion.

Limbaugh benefits from the swirling skepticism and anger. He is the creation—not the creator—of this mood.

BABY BOOMERS

Limbaugh's on-air tone has been described as "Reaganism with a rock 'n' roll beat," and his show has been credited with being the first radio talk program to find a mass following among baby boomers.

In Detroit, for example, Limbaugh's mid-1992 ratings showed him third among all listeners, second among those between the ages of twenty-five and fifty-four, and first among men in that age group. A Detroit radio executive described Limbaugh's success this way: "The story here is that we're now entering the second generation of talk radio listeners—the baby boomers. They have a short attention span. They want to be entertained. They are turning conservative. And Rush is a mirror image of that. He's the one talk show host who instead of being buried by this tidal wave of baby boomers is riding it on a surfboard."[6]

The ratings indicate that Limbaugh is a world champion surfer on a wave rolling across the country. For example, according to an analysis prepared by EFM Media, Limbaugh's syndicator, in late 1991 the show captured more than a twenty share (percentage of radios in use) in Fresno, California, a sixteen share in Rochester, New York, and another sixteen in New Orleans.

As this big population bloc ages, its tastes change and popular culture evolves. For example, information might begin to take precedence over music. As of 1991, news/talk had displaced rock as the sixth most popular format. (The top five are country/western, adult contemporary, top forty, religious, and oldies.)[7]

People like to talk. In New Jersey, Trenton station WKXW switched from adult contemporary to talk at about the time the legislature passed Governor Jim Florio's controversial tax increase. The station was flooded with calls—the size of its audience doubled, and its standing in the central New Jersey ratings went from eighth to first place. That meant a comparable rise in ad revenues. Such changes do not go unnoticed by other station managers thinking about converting to or expanding talk format.

Another apparent factor in the growth of talk radio's constituency is its expansion beyond the middle class. Talk show hosts report increasing numbers of calls from car-phones, which generally belong to corporate managers or others in higher income ranges. When car-phone ownership spreads, the drive-time talk show probably will become even more popular because more of its audience will be able to participate as callers, not just listeners.

TALK RADIO AUDIENCES

Talk radio has been portrayed recently as a political institution dominated by conservative hosts (such as Limbaugh) whose proselytizing turns their listeners into right-wing zealots. A 1993 study by the Times Mirror Center for The People and The Press offers evidence that this judgment is misleadingly simplistic in several respects.[8]

The talk radio audience—especially its members who have actually called in to voice their opinions—*is* disproportionately conservative. Half of all the conservatives surveyed and 37 percent of liberals say they listen regularly or sometimes, and conservatives are twice as likely to be regular listeners as are liberals.

Also surveyed were 112 talk show hosts. They say the people who call their shows represent the public at large, but they also describe their callers as more likely to be conservative, angry, antigovernment, and critical of the president and Congress.

The Center found that Bill Clinton's performance received a negative rating from 53 percent of these radio participants, and a positive rating from only 38 percent. In May 1993, when this survey was conducted, nationwide opinion about the president's job performance was 43 percent disapproving, 39 percent approving.

The survey also found that despite Rush Limbaugh's dominating presence in the talk radio world, talk show hosts collectively are more moderate than are their listeners. For example, more than two-thirds of talk show listeners and callers say they are conservative or lean conservative, but only 46 percent of hosts classify themselves that way.

This split is apparent in attitudes about issues and political personalities. For instance, proposals to allow gays and lesbians to serve in the military were supported by 63 percent of hosts but only 30 percent of regular listeners. Only 39 percent of hosts favored a constitutional amendment to allow school prayer, while 72 percent of their listeners supported the idea. On some issues, such as Congressional term limits, hosts and audiences are closer. That proposal was supported by 70 percent of hosts and 77 percent of listeners.

The study also says talk show hosts are more liberal than the general public about freedom of expression. For instance, 52 percent of the public respondents agree that "books that contain dangerous ideas should be banned from public school libraries," but 89 percent of talk show hosts *disagree* with that position.

Opinions about Ross Perot also substantially differed: 65 percent of listeners liked him, but only 39 percent of hosts agreed. As further evidence that the talk show hosts are far from uniformly conservative, those surveyed said they voted for Clinton over Bush and Perot by a 39 to 23 to 18 percent margin.

The Center's survey does much to dispel the notion that talk radio is a right-wing monolith. The listeners are predominantly conservative, but this study found no evidence that they are mindlessly surrendering their political independence to rabid ideologues who are presiding over talk shows. In fact, the more liberal views of the hosts serve as ballast, stabilizing the programs' content.

Talk show devotees—especially the callers—happen to be the people who care enough to take advantage of these forums and make their opinions heard. To denigrate their activism—regardless of their politics—is to be snobbishly anti-democratic.

Perhaps a larger issue than the callers' views themselves is the way they are treated by news media. The Times Mirror report says "these new voices of public opinion can caricature discontent with American political institutions, rather than genuinely reflect public disquiet." News organizations and politicians tend to read too much into talk-show comments, mistaking loud anger for representativeness.

If the news media treat talk radio comments as definitive evidence of public opinion, they might be creating a self-fulfilling prophecy. When news reports say, "This is the prevailing opinion," people might accept it as such, and an artificial consensus might be born.

CONSERVATIVE CONSPIRACY?

Limbaugh dismisses notions about a conservative talk show conspiracy, claiming that the "dominant media culture"—as reflected by network newscasts and other "mainstream" programming—is skewed to the liberal side, so any conservative influence provides much-needed balance.

On his daily program, Limbaugh frequently receives calls from people who say something like,

"Last night on CBS, I saw this ridiculous story about prison inmates not being treated well enough, and I'm fed up with the news media supporting that kind of coddling." Limbaugh will then deliver an impassioned soliloquy agreeing with and expanding on his caller's theme. Of course, neither will mention that the CBS story they're so agitated about is merely a report about what is happening; it is not an editorial by the network.

But perception is important, and part of Limbaugh's influence is derived from many Americans' perception that news organizations advocate as well as report. Limbaugh says: "The profound anger and distrust of our political institutions felt by so many Americans now includes 'The Media' as well. When people say they feel betrayed and sold out by the old-line political institutions of the country, they include The Media in the mix. The Media is now considered just another part of the arrogant, condescending, elite, and out-of-touch political structure which has ignored the people and their concerns and interests. People are beginning to view the media not as a watchdog against governmental abuses of power but as an institution which is itself engaging in the abuse of power."[9]

Commonly accepted anecdotal evidence suggests that Limbaugh is right about the public's mood, but the Times Mirror study found people to be better disposed toward the news media than Limbaugh thinks they are. Network TV news was rated favorably by 81 percent of the general public and 78 percent of talk show listeners, while talk show hosts gave it only a 54 percent favorable rating. Opinions about daily newspapers break out almost exactly the same way.

Nevertheless, Limbaugh pounds away, counterattacking every time he learns of a news story about the supposedly insidious influence of talk shows. "To the Media Elite," he says, "we may be the disfavored stepchild, but to others, we're setting the standard."

A MEDIA ALTERNATIVE

In 1992, the influence of Limbaugh and the talk-show genre increased substantially in several ways. First, as Limbaugh's soaring ratings indicated, audiences wanted diverse sources of information and opinion, and so were turning to talk shows as supplement or alternative to regular news programs. Similarly, politicians looking to find new ways to reach voters began relying on talk shows to deliver their messages.

George Putnam, a sixty-year broadcasting veteran and host of "Talk Back" on Los Angeles station KIEV, says, "People are dying to speak, and we of talk radio are the only media that has its finger on the pulse of America." He adds that candidates benefit from the talk show format, which is one of "informality and accessibility."[10]

That is one of the most important attributes of talk shows. Members of the audience feel they have a direct link to the host and guest. They consider themselves to be true participants, even if they are just listening, not calling and talking. This differs from news programs, paid candidate broadcasts, advertising spots, and other standard ways of reaching voters. With these formats, the audience is very much on the outside, removed from whatever is going on.

Candidates' increased use of talk programs in 1992 was part of trend toward expanded, decentralized political communication. Instead of having their messages chopped into terse sound bites, the candidates were able to present themselves in a relatively unfiltered way to voters. And because talk hosts often lack the ability or inclination to be tough on their guests, politicians knew they had come upon a valuable way to avoid running the journalistic gauntlet.

Also, candidates found an ever-expanding number of outlets for reaching the public. By election day 1992, fifty-six million American homes— 61 percent of the country—were wired for cable, and received an average of sixty channels.

Talk show popularity was enhanced in 1992 because news organizations found themselves covering talk-show hosts' discussions with the likes of Bill Clinton or Ross Perot. This additional publicity multiplied the impact of those appearances.

For example, Clinton's celebrated saxophone playing on "The Arsenio Hall Show" was seen that night by relatively few people because that program has only so-so ratings. But the next night, an audience of thirty million Americans saw excerpts from the Hall show on the network newscasts.

Limbaugh was a partial player in this process. His show was an enormously popular vehicle for voters who wanted to discuss issues and who enjoyed his relentless conservatism, but he has a policy of no guests. He made exceptions for George Bush and Dan Quayle, but otherwise kept the spotlight focused exclusively on himself, which he and his audience prefer.

He did, however, take note of talk radio's emergence as a visible political force. "Talk media," he said, "is to the dominant media institutions what Ross Perot is to the dominant political institutions. It is the portion of the media that the people trust the most."[11]

One reason people trust these alternatives to news is that they are frustrated by the press corps' persistent emphasis on scandal and insider, "horse-race" politics rather than on issues that affect average Americans' lives. This precipitated, in the words of *Newsweek*'s Jonathan Alter, "two rebellions at once...a rebellion against politics as usual and a rebellion against media as usual."[12]

Media critic Jon Katz says of 1992: "Never was it clearer that journalism and the electorate have radically different agendas. Reporters, determined to function as a sort of campaign FBI, were obsessed to the end with sex, lies, and transcripts, scrambling to catch candidates with their memos and their pants down—alleged mistresses, Iran-Contra, decades-old draft letters. It was the public—not the media—that pressed concerns about the economy, women's issues, health care, race, and poverty."[13]

Smart politicians recognized the importance of this public disaffection. In Bill Clinton's case, his ability to do an end run around the regular political press corps might have saved his candidacy. Early in the summer, Clinton was facing a virtual news blackout because of journalists' fascination with the Perot candidacy. Some polls showed Clinton dropping into third place as voters either forgot about him or remembered only the negatives that had received so much attention during the early primaries.

One of his media consultants, Mandy Grunwald, advocated using a "pop-culture strategy" to counter the noncoverage. She saw radio as the key to redefining Clinton's image. Every major city, she said, has a much listened-to drive-time show and a serious political program. The campaign should get Clinton on one of these every day. She noted that "some people say these kinds of things are 'unpresidential.' Bull. This is how people get information." [14]

Grunwald later said she became intrigued by this approach when a chambermaid at a Wisconsin hotel told Clinton: "I saw you on 'Donahue.' You were great." To Grunwald, the maid didn't seem to be the political junkie type—someone who would regularly read newspaper accounts about the ins and outs of campaigning. She was relating to Clinton as person more than politician.

Talk shows allow the personal to outshine the political. Grunwald reasoned there must be plenty more potential voters like that maids out there among the non-news-addicted public.[15]

Clinton used these appearances successfully, presenting himself as a "good guy" with a sense of humor and innovative policy ideas. Even New York's combative Don Imus gave "redneck Bozo" Clinton credit for having a sense of humor. As Grunwald had realized, removing the news media's filter would let her candidate project a far more appealing image than most of the public had so far seen.

Later in the race, Clinton's tacticians found even more ways to use radio. For instance, they set up an 800 number with a voice mail menu that could feed radio actualities—sound bites from Clinton or his surrogates—to radio stations throughout the country. They duplicated this national operation in many of their state headquarters. Eventually, they were delivering broadcast-ready messages to twenty-two hundred radio stations daily.[16]

Republican strategists, like many other politicians, were not sure where the real power was to be found on the rapidly changing map of media avenues to the public. They belatedly realized they were not taking full advantage of talk shows. They courted Limbaugh, knowing that his program would be one of the best vehicles for reaching the conservative constituents who were unenthusiastic about Bush, but whose support was absolutely essential if the president was to win a second term. Dan Quayle—more popular than Bush among some of the GOP's conservative true believers—appeared on Limbaugh's show in July to tout Bush, blast the Democratic Congress, and reiterate his own stance on "family values," which was the basis for his duel with TV's fictive "Murphy Brown."

A COMMUNICATIONS GAP

Reminders cropped up throughout the campaign about the gap between the news media's and the public's judgments about what is newsworthy. Anyone interested in the public's agenda should have been paying attention to subjects dominating talk radio on any given day.

On Thursday, February 20—two days after a New Hampshire primary that reflected a striking absence of consensus about whom voters wanted to be president—Ross Perot appeared on Larry King's national television talk show and wedged open the door to a presidential candidacy. His approval of a petition drive to put him on all fifty states' ballots would turn out to be one of the defining events of the political year.

The next day, news media response was minimal. The top producers at ABC News, for example, didn't even mention Perot as they planned the day's coverage. On Saturday, the *Los Angeles Times* ran an item on page eighteen. Two weeks later, the *New York Times* and United Press International offered small items about Perot's Dallas telephone banks. The *Washington Post* didn't run a story until late March.[17] Although an earthquake was rumbling, journalistic seismographs weren't picking it up.

But talk radio was. In Hartford, Connecticut, WTIC talk show host Michael Harrison hadn't seen the King show and didn't know much about Perot, but on February 21, Perot was what most of his callers wanted to talk about.

The same thing happened on local talk shows around the country: Wilmington, Delaware; Wichita, Kansas; Seattle; Los Angeles; and elsewhere. As days passed and the mainstream news media still reported nothing, talk radio became Perot's mainstream. Callers no longer were just asking about Perot, they were announcing organizational meetings of Perot volunteers and urging listeners to attend. By late March, when serious press coverage of Perot began, he had reached 20 percent in the polls. Talk radio was the principal medium that got him there.[18]

The Perot story is not an isolated case. In the aftermath of the Los Angeles riots in May, ABC anchorman Peter Jennings recognized the gap between what his news organization was delivering and what people were thinking. An ABC special centering on President Bush's post-riot address to the nation followed the same old formula: after the president, offer some "balance" from an established spokesman, in this case, NAACP president Benjamin Hooks, who said what he always said. The next day, Jennings listened to a local New York talk show on an African-American radio station and realized that the network had become so enamored of safe predictability that it had missed reporting the true public mood.[19] Talk radio—not network news—was delivering reality.

OUT OF TOUCH

While mainstream media honchos belatedly realized that they were out of touch with the public, Limbaugh could chortle at their surprise and critique their scrambling as they tried to figure out what was going on. The issue as he saw it was more than a question of journalistic competence. Of course, the major news organizations had missed the Perot boat. Of course they didn't know what most Americans were thinking. All this fit in with two of his favorite theories: "The dominant media culture is composed of liberals who seek to push their view on society without admitting they are doing it," and, "Conservatives are indeed the silent majority in this country...."[20]

In other words, a media establishment dominated by liberals could not even hope to understand the sentiments of a conservative country. Also, the Limbaugh argument goes, by being so blindly intent on advancing their agenda, these liberals are sure not to notice even profound shifts in public opinion.

Limbaugh's judgment about the dominance of conservatism is certainly debatable. The United States is so diverse in so many aspects that it does not lend itself to nice, neat collective labeling.

Ross Perot, like Limbaugh, was a from-out-of-nowhere superstar of 1992. He gets mixed treatment from Limbaugh. In one interview, Limbaugh praised Perot as the only candidate who didn't run away from difficult issues. But Limbaugh also made clear his dislike of what he considered to be Perot's manipulation of people who in good faith—and sometimes at considerable cost—supported him.

Part of Limbaugh's distaste for Perot might come from Limbaugh's realizing that the talk show medium he helped make so potent had in turn helped give birth to the Perot candidacy. In *The Way Things Ought to Be*, Limbaugh labels as "pure deceit" Perot's claims about running for president only because of spontaneous public demands that he do so. Limbaugh also says Perot fails the character test that presidents must meet: "He made promise after promise [to his supporters], then broke them all."

A FAIR HEARING

The aspirations of Limbaugh and a horde of politicians all came together in 1992, linked by the popularity and power of talk shows. While the politicians were trying to win elections, Limbaugh was trying to be a successful broadcaster and, secondarily, to present political views that he thought were not receiving a fair hearing.

He takes issue with those who claim that he and other talk show hosts wield too much influence. Limbaugh says, "Contrary to the fears of many in the mainstream media...radio talk show hosts cannot and do not invent public emotion." He cites the 1989 Congressional pay raise as an example of public furor on talk shows merely delaying, not preventing, government action. And he notes that the latter-day version of the Boston Tea Party—people sending tea bags to members of Congress to protest the pay hike—was the idea of a talk show caller, not a host.

During the House Bank rubber check scandal, Limbaugh did urge his listeners to demand specific action—the release of the names of members who had written bad checks. The names eventually were released, but Limbaugh applied only one of many stimuli to this process. Extensive news coverage of this instance of congressional irresponsibility already had the public up in arms. Limbaugh dismisses those who credit him for getting the names released: "The American people did that. I just helped amplify their outrage."

EXPANDING UNIVERSE

Part of politicians' eagerness to use talk shows comes from their recognition of realignments occurring in the media universe. Not too many years ago, most people, when asked about the pre-eminent information sources, would say the *New York Times*, *Time*, and CBS News, or some minor variation on that line-up. A few years later, the monopoly of influence had given way to intense competition in the top ranks. Other news organizations raised their aspirations and improved their work: add *The Washington Post*, *U.S. News and World Report*, and ABC, among others, to the mix. Technological advances, including wiring most of the country for cable, have kept the list expanding.

By 1992, the icons of "old news" no longer had the clout to influence the political agenda as they once had. The new technology was fostering "new news," reaching constituencies that previously had been mostly ignored. For example, even MTV (Music Television) jumped into campaign coverage, with its rising star of political journalism Tabitha Soren presiding over efforts to "Rock the Vote."

Like Soren, Limbaugh was a member of the new, expanded roster of gatekeepers, supplementing if not superseding Peter, Dan, Tom, and other traditional arbiters of political information.

As new faces appeared, so too did the mechanisms of mass communication keep evolving. The television facet of this expansion elicits varied reactions. Those who look at it from a revenue standpoint despair. They see the pie remaining the same size, while the number of increasingly smaller slices multiplies. But for the consumer of information, the more slices the better; diversity is wonderful.

The money people respond by acquiring additional slices; for example, NBC created a cable sibling, CNBC. The viewer, meanwhile, has remarkable opportunities to acquire information, not only from CNN, C-SPAN, and other national cable sources, but also from local stations that avail themselves of satellite-relayed material and other benefits of advanced technology.

While the television industry reconfigures itself, radio adjusts to deregulation. That has intensified competition, because the market will not sustain an infinite number of stations. There are only so many listeners and advertisers to go around. Many radio stations are struggling to survive. In the Darwinian world of broadcasting, a shake-out of weaker stations is inevitable.

Add to all this the explosive growth in computer networking and the availability of fax machines. These offer yet more ways for people to get a diverse array of facts and opinions.

AN ALTERNATIVE

Public wariness about journalism stems in part from the blurring of the line between news and entertainment. That wariness and that blurring work to Limbaugh's advantage. He can offer himself as an alternative to "dominant media" that many in his audience consider untrustworthy. And when he makes his pronouncements about candidates, issues, and news items, he can dress them up in the finery of entertainment—jokes, songs, sound effects, and whatnot—without seeming outrageously beyond the pale.

After all, many people rely on Jay Leno's monologue, David Letterman's "Top Ten" lists, and "Saturday Night Live" impersonations for more than humor. Viewers use these performances as part of their opinion-building process. Certainly they differentiate between the reliability of what they hear from Jay Leno and what Dan Rather says, but that differentiation might not be as substantial as news professionals like to think it is.

Dissatisfied with the standard fare of politics and journalism, the mass audience is unlikely to expect or want old-fashioned, straight-down-the-middle

packaging of information. Limbaugh's idiosyn-
cratic style suits them just fine. He falls somewhere
in between Leno and Rather, coming across to
many as worth taking seriously even when he is
being funny.

TAKING THE PLUNGE

By the end of the 1992 presidential race, all the
candidates had plunged into the talk show pool.
Bush, Clinton, and Perot had appeared a total of
ninety-six times on five major television programs
that had not before been standard venues for presidents and would-be presidents: "Larry King Live,"
"Donahue," "CBS This Morning," ABC's "Good
Morning, America," and NBC's "Today."[21] They
also turned up on dozens of other national and
local talk programs.

While talk shows became recognized as
crucial campaign battlegrounds, Limbaugh did
his best to offset what he considered to be the
increasingly pro-Clinton tilt of news coverage. He
championed the conservative cause, often more

convincingly than Bush did, and attacked Clinton as an untrustworthy ultraliberal. This partisanship did not turn off Limbaugh's listeners; throughout 1992 his audience grew. Although George Bush failed to make a winning case for continuing his presidency, Limbaugh emerged from the political wars triumphant.

The conclusion of the 1992 campaign by no means marked the end of talk shows' political clout. Bill Clinton probably wishes it had.

A series of missteps and controversial moves during the first months of his presidency produced political headaches made more throbbing by talk programs. One survey of talk radio hosts found that Clinton was being more heavily criticized than even Saddam Hussein had been during the Gulf War, earning the president the title of "most bashed individual in talk radio history" from one show host.[22]

Clinton aides knew they were being battered and blamed it in part on the relentless torrent of information flooding the public. One

White House staff member said: "We're wired in real time now. People hear something and immediately react without reflection, without comparing what Rush Limbaugh says to, say, what Dan Rather says. They can wing in with faxes and telegrams and calls based only on Limbaugh, and for many he is the sole source of information."[23]

Limbaugh gleefully watched the chaos. Although he certainly would prefer to have a Republican president, he knew the Clinton gaffes were manna from political heaven. Issues such as the mishandled nomination of Zoe Baird for attorney general and the proposals about gays in the military were perfect for Limbaugh's fulminating and his listeners' ire.

Whether the calls went to the likes of Limbaugh or C-SPAN's studiously neutral Brian Lamb or Washington, D.C.'s liberal Diane Rehm, an underlying theme behind the callers' words was a desire to be heard, to participate. Talk show power had been established during the previous year's campaign; the public liked it, and now it was expanding.

The steady advance of technology helps. Some mobile phone services offer one-button access to call-in show numbers. United Airlines announced plans to carry Larry King's program live on planes equipped with telephones. Audience and access can be expected to keep growing.

Recognizing this, the Clinton administration has designed strategies to make talk programming work for them. For instance, in September 1993, when Vice President Al Gore unveiled his plan for cutting government waste, he made the rounds of talk shows: NBC's "Today" to answer viewers' called-in questions, and "Donahue" to chat with host and audience. He even appeared on David Letterman's "Late Show" to trade jokes, offering a "top ten" list of reasons to like being Vice President and donning goggles to illustrate how the government tests the sturdiness of its glass ashtrays.

With this approach, Gore certainly reached a larger audience than he would have had he relied solely on C-SPAN and "Meet the Press." But some cautionary words were heard. Bob Lichter, director for the Center for Media and Public Affairs said: "I'm not sure I want to have a vice president who I can imagine interviewing Zsa Zsa Gabor at 11:30 at night. In narrow terms, Gore performed very well. He humanized himself. My qualms are that in the long run, the power of the presidency depends on a certain larger-than-life aura. And popular culture shrinks that aura. It's telling people at the outset this isn't serious; it's all a joke."[24]

Lichter's point is well-taken. Politicians could become so enamored of talk programs that they overly adjust the style and content of their work to meet that medium's demands. Consider the frightening prospect of Al Gore acting as Ed McMahon to Bill Clinton's Johnny Carson.

Even if this specter never appears, politicians might glide farther down the slippery slope of sound-bite-filled campaigning and governing, just switching from newscast glibness to talk show glibness. That might initially please the entertainment-addicted masses, but entertaining governance is not necessarily good governance.

REACHING THE VOTERS

The 1990s' version of talk radio has galvanized voters—so far, principally conservatives—in a way that might not have been possible without a medium that gave its audience a sense of being participants, not mere spectators.

This is truly the perfect vehicle for Limbaugh's temperament and talents. He possesses both the entertainer's and the politician's abilities to determine what an audience wants. When he figures that out, he knows how to turn it into a product that entertains while remaining intrinsically political.

The rise of talk radio should encourage all who favor opening up the political process. Even liberals can take heart, because nothing inherent in the talk format's popularity makes it exclusively the conservatives' domain. Like much else in politics, the dominance of particular ideology in talk radio might be cyclical. Somewhere out there, the liberal version of Rush Limbaugh might be polishing his or her talk show skills. And the liberal counterparts of Limbaugh's legions might be awaiting their champion. Who knows?

In any event, talk shows are helping Americans think about issues and about those who govern. Rush Limbaugh and his colleagues in this business—regardless of where they perch on the political spectrum—deserve some credit for making that happen.

DELIVERING
THE GOODS

7

The medium itself is nothing.

To be anything more than just another surge of sound coming across the airwaves, talk radio must have content worth caring about and an audience willing to care.

It also needs a host able to make topics radio-friendly. This means relying on words alone, no pictures—a difficult task in the era of television's rapid-fire video and *USA Today*'s eye-arresting graphics.

Rush Limbaugh has a showman's finely tuned appreciation of what makes a talk program work. With his usual modesty, he says his radio show is a "unique blend of humor, irreverence, and the serious discussion of events with a conservative slant. Nowhere else in the media today will you find all these ingredients in one presentation." No carefully thought through strategy produced this formula, says Limbaugh. "It was just me being myself. I like to have fun, I like being irreverent, and I am dead serious about the things I feel passionately."

He also says: "The show is devoted exclusively to what I think. I do not attempt to find out what the people of the country are thinking." He contends that it is "the height of presumptuousness" for talk show hosts to believe they can discover what people think "by virtue of what happens on their show."[1]

That is a bit disingenuous, because Limbaugh also says that "people were going crazy over this show, primarily because of my political point of view," and he regularly asserts that he, not "the dominant media," is truly in touch with what the *real* majority of Americans *really* thinks.

He knows that millions of people trust and sometimes act upon his pronouncements, and he pledges to be unwaveringly honest. But he offers as a bottom line, "Still, I am first a broadcaster, bound by the dictates and requirements of broadcasting," which of course means he must win and hold an audience large enough to turn a profit. In his case, he has his eye on substantial profit. His 1992 earnings have been estimated at $12 million[2], and could be considerably more in 1993.

Limbaugh was clearly delighted when some opponent called him "the most dangerous man in America." He adopted the label and wears it, along with the sobriquet "the Godzilla of broadcasting," as a badge of honor.

He also has standards that must be met by callers who want air time on his show. They must be passionate and interesting enough to hold the attention of listeners. Limbaugh says: "Remember, this is a business, not some boring public service foray. I must attract an audience, not send them off to other stations." He knows that people who take the trouble to call constitute only a tiny percentage of his overall audience. He plays principally to this larger mass rather than catering to the callers.

Limbaugh displays an interesting ambivalence about his politics. He certainly is a passionate conservative, but his main goal is to be a successful broadcaster. The two interests can conflict. One of the principal tenets he advances in *The Way Things Ought to Be* is, "My success is not determined by who wins elections; my success is determined by how many listeners I have."

This means that when he embarks on his daily "excursions into broadcast excellence," he cares less about advancing a conservative agenda than about doing "the best damn radio show I can do." That is because, he says, he wants those listeners to come back, day after day.

NOT JUST AVERAGE FOLK

Talk show hosts might have a profound effect on the discourse and political thinking of millions of "average Americans," but the hosts themselves are not just average folk.

According to the 1993 study conducted by the Times Mirror Center for The People and The

Press, these are some characteristics of talk show hosts:

- They are well-educated; 60 percent have a college degree, compared to 21 percent of the general public.

- They are relatively wealthy; 33 percent make $50,000-$100,000, and 30 percent make more than $100,000.

- They are relatively nonreligious; 30 percent of the hosts say they have no religious affiliation, compared to 10 percent of the public.

When asked if those listeners who actually call in are representative of the general public in their area, 56 percent of the hosts say yes, while 38 percent say the callers are unrepresentative. More specifically, they say the following groups are the most under-represented: feminists, liberals, pro-choice, and racially tolerant. The groups most over-represented are these: people who are angry, conservatives, Clinton-bashers, and those who are generally antigovernment.

A bare majority of the hosts say their audiences (not just the callers) share the prevalent ideology of the general public in their area, while 34 percent say their listeners are more conservative, and 13 percent say more liberal.

Despite Limbaugh's attempts to downplay his influence on public opinion, almost two-thirds of the hosts in the Times Mirror survey said they believed they often play an important role in shaping opinion, and three-quarters could cite a recent case when they had seen such impact. The most frequently mentioned examples involved focusing public attention on local issues, influencing local elections, letting public officials know what the public was thinking, and pointing out government corruption.

These survey results are important in understanding the talk genre beyond Limbaugh's own show. Although Limbaugh is the dominant figure in this broadcast field, the institution of talk radio clearly is not limited by either Limbaugh's personal style, his politics, or his approach to his professional responsibilities as a broadcaster.

CASTING A WARY EYE

Michael Deaver, who cultivated Ronald Reagan's image during the first years of his presidency, watches the rise of talk media with a knowing eye. He says that Rush Limbaugh, Larry King, Phil Donahue, and other show hosts provide their audiences with "a way to get in." On the other hand, says Deaver, the networks, along with most of the political process, operate as closed clubs, disenfranchising people.[3]

This is part of the case that defines talk programming as an asset to democracy, a vehicle for citizen participation in public debate. It is not a universally held viewpoint.

A March 1993 editorial in the liberal magazine *The Nation* notes that call-in shows derive much of their popularity from "real problems of democracy: the restriction of popular participation in decision making and access to government and corporate authority." But emerging from "class resentment and mass alienation" can come a "capacity for bashing unpopular minorities.

The talk show demagogues are adept at manipulating anger and turning righteous resentment into fearful hatred of the oppressed. That, indeed, is a constant danger in any democratic system, but in more modulated forums—legislatures, town meetings, public hearings, Op-Ed pages—there is space and time for the devel opment of coalitions, compromises and sometimes even common sense."

This editorial made the point that "the Rush Limbaughs of the world should not be censored." Rather, political leaders should be more willing to enter the fray, explaining and defending their policies and not abandoning the field to Limbaugh and his colleagues.

This means going where the people are— using talk programs. Given Limbaugh's general unwillingness to make exceptions to his no-guest policy, Larry King has become the preeminent figure in providing politicians with talk show air time. A few officials, such as New York Governor Mario Cuomo, host their own occasional talk programs.

The Nation's editorial about this politician-public linkage concludes: "If audiences are treated as solicitously as voters, their anger apprehended and their concerns discussed, they will respond with more respect. After all, today's mob was yesterday's electorate."

Talk radio can play an important role during times of national or community upheaval. For instance, during the 1992 trial in the Rodney King case and the Los Angeles riots that followed the police officers' acquittal, racial tensions increased alarmingly in many cities.

Fear and hatred grow fastest in the dark, so it was important to keep a spotlight shining on the underlying causes of discontent. In practical terms, this spotlight sometimes takes the form of conversation.

When people are talking to each other, understanding of differing viewpoints increases and tension might diminish. Airing concerns can be cathartic. Discussion might take place face-to-face or electronically. The conversation can be direct or mediated by someone such as a talk show host. The format is not as important as is sustaining the dialogue.

But talk can also take nasty turns. Those public forums that might help thoughtfulness prevail can also fuel hate. One of the worst cases is the "Race and Reason" talk show that has appeared on some public access cable TV channels. It is a vehicle for Tom Metzger and the White Aryan Resistance, a particularly vicious racist organization. An Oregon court imposed a $12.5 million judgment against Metzger and WAR for inciting skinheads to murder an Ethiopian man in Portland in 1988.

Even in mainstream programming, the potential exists for spreading hate. For instance, suppose that during a time of exceptional racial tension, talk shows fill the air waves with callers' exhortations to "Shoot the niggers" and "Shoot the honkies." Some listeners might find their own fear or anger rising to match that of the callers.

This is when responsible talk show hosts are essential. They should either screen out the most inflammatory calls, or take it upon themselves to make the case for reason.

Merely turning over the airwaves to those who foment violence is unacceptable. It cannot be justified as "letting everyone have his or her say," or as an exercise of Constitutionally guaranteed free expression. "Shoot the niggers" is not protected free speech any more than is Justice Holmes's famous example of shouting fire in a crowded theater when there is no fire.

Controlling access in this way is important, but perhaps not as much as is exercising the moral suasion that some talk show hosts command. Limbaugh, for example, apparently is deeply trusted by many of his listeners. On any given day, he will receive calls from people who say, "I never really understood what's at stake in the abortion debate until you explained it," or "You're the only one who really knows what that gun control legislation would do to the country." About this, Limbaugh says, "I am quite aware that millions of people invest their trust in my honesty, and I will never be cavalier about that."

Although his critics might find little to cheer in that, even most of them would have to admit that Limbaugh is not a hater. He does not advocate violence or allow others to do so on his program.

Calls to Limbaugh's show are well-screened. Volume makes that necessary, but so does Limbaugh's desire not to give free advertising to people, products, or causes that he does not care for. Does that controlled access mean his show features only a limited number of topics and viewpoints? Of course. Does it mean only people who agree with Limbaugh get on the air? No; even though Limbaugh might worry more about dullness than unfairness, callers *can* get on the air and argue with him. Does this screening keep the lunatic fringe—skinheads and the like—from having a priceless forum for dispensing their hate-filled messages? Yes.

The medium is so innately powerful that common sense safeguards must be imposed on its content. The skilled talk show host will, most of the time, have a significant advantage in conversation or debate. After all, this is a *job* for these people; they talk for a living every day. If they decide to compete with a caller in cleverness or rhetorical technique, they usually will win. But that would prove nothing. (Limbaugh sometimes turns aside callers who launch into obviously well-practiced mini-speeches. Limbaugh says, "Here's someone else angling for a show of his own," and quickly moves on.)

Although Limbaugh prides himself on being well-removed from extremism, not everyone shares that perception of him.

For example, he takes great offense at being called a racist. On one fall afternoon in 1993, he engaged in a prolonged and loud debate on his radio show with an African-American woman caller who said that is exactly what he is. He retorted that the charge was "infantile," among other things. His anger obviously growing, he said, "Because I'm white, I'm automatically racist and automatically disqualified" from commenting about Rodney King or other race-related matters. He then went into a long anticrime speech and said, "I'm sick and tired of being called a racist" because some of the people he wants locked up are black. And, for good measure, he criticized the civil rights movement as exemplifying racism.

This was vintage Limbaugh. He steered the discussion from race to the safer terrain of crime, and tried to define the terms of debate in such a way that if he could establish himself as being anti-crime, then he must not be a racist. That logic follows a tortuous path, but he presented it with such angry eloquence that he must have evoked thunderous applause in Rush Rooms around the country.

Limbaugh did, however, make some valid points that his caller had trouble refuting. She said, for example, that he had defended the police officers who had been convicted of beating Rodney King. He said he never had, and she could cite no time or specifics otherwise. To give Limbaugh his due, he is frequently attacked by callers who accuse him of various evils, but then have no specific quotations or other evidence to back up the charges.

But Limbaugh has not always been able to stroll away from controversy that he has generated. After the Gay and Lesbian Alliance Against Defamation protested about some of his references to AIDS patients and homosexuals, Limbaugh apologized, although he claims he is merely politically opposed to "the militant homosexual agenda" and doesn't "care who sleeps with whom."

OUT OF SYNCH

Even experienced talk show hosts sometimes find themselves out of synch with their audience, as

Phil Donahue learned during the 1992 presidential campaign.

With Bill Clinton as his guest, Donahue decided the day's topic should be the candidate's alleged marital infidelity. He resurrected the Gennifer Flowers story and asked Clinton about "suspicions fueled by allegations." Clinton told him, basically, that his marriage was none of Donahue's business.

But the host persisted. The audience then made itself heard, applauding when Clinton told Donahue certain questions were out of bounds and when he said, "I don't believe I or any other decent human being should have to put up with the kind of questioning you're putting me through." When Donahue went into the audience for questions, one woman took the microphone and said: "I think, given the pathetic state of most of the United States at this point…I can't believe you spent half an hour of airtime attacking this man's character. I'm not even a Bill Clinton supporter, but I think this is ridiculous." The rest of the audience cheered and applauded.[4]

Journalists covering the campaign, although certainly not above shoveling sleaze themselves, saw this kind of episode as proof of talk shows' lack of substance. Political columnists Jack Germond and Jules Witcover said Donahue, for instance, was a "scandalmonger masquerading as journalist" whose "bread and butter was sensationalism, but who sought to lacquer it with a veneer of serious demeanor."

Donahue seemed somewhat chastened by seeing his fans' adoration turn sour. A few days later, when Clinton made another appearance on the show, this time with fellow candidate Jerry Brown, Donahue backed off altogether, letting the two debate without interruption. This produced one of the best exchanges of the entire campaign.

Sometimes less is more.

POWER OF TALK RADIO

Despite its history dating back to the medium's early days, talk radio is still finding its way among the forces of power in American society. Its recent surge in popularity and concurrent increase in influence have not always been matched by comparable levels of ethical behavior.

Bob Ray Sanders is a veteran Texas television journalist who recently has hosted a talk radio program with a popular Dallas station. He says: "Talk radio's greatest failure is that it has not had a calming effect instead of being incendiary. It's more natural for us to be the yellers and screamers, the provocateurs."

An African-American in a community with perpetually tense race relations, Sanders says, "Particularly in crisis, people turn to us." He cites one instance in early 1993, when racial violence followed the Dallas Cowboys victory parade through the city's downtown. Anger and frustration were high, and no systemic process existed to relieve them. "I had one caller—a young black man—who said he was ready to go out and shoot somebody. I kept him on the line for a long time. Later he called back and told me, 'You stopped me from doing something crazy.'"

Provocateur or peacemaker? Dispassionate observer or compassionate participant? The talk host might like to stay removed and avoid making such choices, but the heat of events melts down cool abstraction.

Should Sanders have told the young man who wanted to shoot someone that it was none of his concern, that he was merely a talk show host? That caller had not seen Sanders as someone removed from the issue at hand, but rather as someone to be trusted and listened to.

By soliciting opinion and shaping dialogue, talk show hosts influence events. Attempts to disengage and profess neutrality would ring false.

Talk show hosts have been described as the political organizers of the nineties, and their shows as outlets for the energies and emotions of people who have no other political vehicles at their disposal. Even if those who host talk radio had no intention of playing this role, it has been thrust upon them, and they are ethically obligated to wield this power responsibly.

The American Jewish Committee issued *Hate in Talk Radio* in 1991, documenting outrageous behavior (usually racist) by some talk show hosts and offering some suggestions. Among the ideas presented to the industry were these:

- Owners of stations should take seriously their responsibility to serve the public interest. They should seek out and promote talk-radio talents who use their entertainment skills to improve human relations.

- Hosts should study their craft, and see the effective handling of bigotry as a matter of professionalism.

The AJC report also urged community organizations to monitor local stations and challenge those that do not responsibly handle bigotry on the air.

At the heart of this report and similar exhortations to the talk radio industry is that racial and ethnic slurs are not entertainment. Just because they elicit guffaws from bigots does not make them acceptable. Any program or host that has to rely on bigots as the core audience is working against the interests of the community as a whole.

Do talk radio and you are no longer a spectator. The talk show host—be it Rush Limbaugh with six hundred-plus stations or a small-town, small-station disc jockey with a few thousand listeners—is a player.

BIG AUDIENCES, BIG BUCKS

Radio is the principal home of the talk show, but for superstars such as Limbaugh, the bigger audiences and bigger bucks of television are hard to resist.

One observer of the mass media looked at the mix of the confessional and the political, and wrote of these shows, "They amounted to a new kind of media, a modern variant of the old afternoon blue collar tabloid, a hybrid of entertainment and journalism, public affairs and primal scream."[5]

The ranks of show hosts are crowded: Oprah and Phil and Sally and Montel and Geraldo and, seemingly, every other ambulatory man and woman able to hold a microphone and ask intrusive and embarrassing questions.

Particularly when the format is inquisitorial, television has a big advantage over radio—the audience at home can watch the victim squirm. When the objects of scrutiny are left-handed transvestite prostitutes and the mothers who no longer love them, ogling is more important than thinking.

Not all television talk shows are geek parades, at least not of that variety. Of entertainment talk programs, "The Tonight Show" flourished during the Jack Paar and Johnny Carson eras. Its current prospects are more uncertain, mainly because "Tonight's" success has spawned so many imitators.

RELIGIOUS TALK SHOWS
Lodged somewhere between entertainment and public affairs—but occupying their own niche of

controversy—are the religious talk shows. Originating in the early days of radio, they now are commonplace on radio and television, featuring local and national representatives of various denominations. They include the relatively sedate, such as Pat Robertson's "700 Club," which provided exposure and mailing lists extensive enough to be a springboard for its host's 1988 presidential campaign.

During the 1993 gays-in-the-military controversy, Robertson showed he still has political muscle. During one edition of the "700 Club," Robertson criticized the "very, very radical groups" that supported reform of Pentagon policy, and said: "They don't represent many people, but they're so noisy that everybody thinks they do....What should a Christian do? Get on your telephone and dial your congressman or your senator...(202)-224-3121...I think you'll get their attention." He flashed the phone number on the screen several times. That was all he needed to do.

By 5:00 P.M. that day, the Capitol Hill switchboard had received 434,000 calls, ten times the daily average. Most of the callers, not surprisingly, urged representatives to oppose liberalizing the military's policy about gays.[6]

Some programs offer genuine inspiration and comfort. Toward the other end of the spectrum are shows such as those featuring television evangelist Robert Tilton's send-money-and-be-saved exhortations.

Special ethical standards apply to those who produce and host these shows because many audience members are extraordinarily trusting of religious broadcasters. The same people who might resist the blandishments of political talkers will willingly send a check to a huckster who proclaims himself a preacher. Legitimate religious broadcasters respect this and use their influence carefully. Less scrupulous ones understand this too, but turn it to their own ends.

Just as talk radio and television can transform political discourse through oversimplification, so can they undercut the foundations of religion.

Media scholar Neil Postman is particularly unimpressed with television's delivery of religious messages. On TV, he says, "religion, like everything else, is presented, quite simply and without apology, as an entertainment. Everything that makes religion an historic, profound, and sacred human activity is stripped away; there is no ritual, no dogma, no tradition, no theology, and above all, no sense of spiritual transcendence. On these shows, the preacher is tops. God comes out as second banana."[7]

SUNDAY MORNINGS

In news programming, Sunday mornings remain the principal home of staid political talk. Shows such as "Meet the Press" have been on the air ever since television first found a place in American homes.

From pure interviews, the format has changed to encourage banter among participants. For instance, on "This Week With David Brinkley," George Will, Sam Donaldson, and Cokie Roberts interview their guests—assorted members of

Congress, cabinet secretaries, and other muckety-mucks—and then, after the guests have departed, offer their own wisdom to their viewers, while Brinkley acts as avuncular referee. Personal one-upmanship among the journalist/talkers is at least as important as shedding light on an issue.

Some programs dispense with interviews in favor of fast-paced chatter. Substance fades into the background. "The issue: the federal deficit. In five seconds, how do we fix it? The issue: world peace. In five seconds, how do we get it?" If you're not a master of pithy one-liners, you can't play this game.

"The McLaughlin Group," one of the more contentious of these programs has been called "an ideological food fight" by former White House press secretary Jody Powell.

It is not unique. One edition of a similar program, CNN's "Crossfire," featured this exchange between two political sages:

Pat Buchanan: "I don't believe man descended from apes, Tom, but in your case I'll make an exception."

Tom Braden: "You look more like one every day, Pat."[8]

Despite the absence of dignity on such shows, some print journalists have plunged into television talk. They often are astounded by this medium's credibility and impact, and by the celebrity status that accompanies "being on TV." Veteran political columnist Jack Germond says: "You could write your damn fingers off for twenty-five years and never have the same reach as television. Television is just a monster."[9]

Germond and other print journalists who do TV are witnesses and participants in a significant change in the way opinion gets to the public. The talk show is pushing aside the newspaper op-ed page as prime deliverer of commentary.

This has its pluses and minuses. The audience for thought-provoking issues discussion always needs expanding, and television does that. But in conforming to TV's format demands, that discussion sometimes becomes so simplistic as to be meaningless or even misleading.

As is the case with talk radio, the conventional wisdom about TV's political talk shows is that they are conservative-dominated. From the thoughtful discussions on William F. Buckley Jr.'s "Firing Line" to the shooting gallery of John McLaughlin's "The McLaughlin Group," conservatives certainly seem the more visible talk show force.

Some observers have attributed this conservative hegemony to the liberals' tendency to disdain television technique so emphatically that viewers are put off. Their approach seems to be, "I am not a TV star, so you must love me for my ideas." The world doesn't work that way. To do well on this medium requires a willingness to adapt—at least partially—to its demands.

Some liberals venturing into the talk show world also fall into the trap of preaching to the choir rather than trying to win converts. That makes for a small audience. Texan Bob Ray Sanders says, "Liberal talk show hosts are going to have to be outrageous to catch attention of more than just liberals." He counts his own program a success because "the majority of my calls are people who disagree with me." This radio experience applies also to television.

Writing in *The New Yorker* about liberals' befuddled efforts to make talk programs work to their advantage, James Wolcott said: "Liberals walk away from a fight, then wonder why they lost. Lean *into* that microphone if you want to be heard."

LIBERALS REGROUP

Among the liberals willing to do battle on Limbaugh's turf is Jim Hightower, former Texas Agriculture Commissioner and long popular among Democrats for his populist politics and brisk humor. He has begun offering two-minute commentaries (carried, as of late 1993, on fifty stations), and is planning a three-hour syndicated talk show.

Hightower promises to be a "Johnny Appleseed nationally for the progressive viewpoint." He thinks radio offers fertile ground for sowing liberalism.

"The Left's failure," he says, "is that we haven't been in the mainstream on a daily basis." He charges that "the media are dominated by right-wing and corporate orthodoxy."

He says many Americans gravitate to radio commentaries and talk shows because they "feel kicked out of politics—unwanted and uninvolved." Some of these are hard-core Limbaugh fans, but, says Hightower, "there is a constituency wanting to hear a progressive viewpoint day in and day out."

He has studied Limbaugh's success: "Limbaugh is an unabashed spokesman and a very entertaining spokesman for the far-right constituency." Hightower says he doesn't want to become the "liberal Limbaugh" because he thinks that would mean being consistently negative. "I'm a political missionary," he says, "and I don't want to be a left-wing ranter."

He does, however, want to be "competitive for hearts and minds." He praises radio as "a very democratic little box" and says he can stay in tune with the public—at least the liberal public—through his "pulse taking at the Chat and Chew Cafe," a Texas version of Garrison Keillor's Lake Wobegon hangouts.

OUT WITH OBJECTIVITY

Liberals should take note of an important change in media standards: Objectivity is no longer an across-the-board requirement for on-air product. Limbaugh is among those who realize that efforts to balance perfectly every discussion of every issue are likely to produce audience-losing dullness. Although a solid case remains for no-compromise objectivity as the goal of pure news programs, talk show standards need not be so rigid.

Some media professionals rejoice in the liveliness that can result from the more flexible approach. Terry Heaton, news director at a North Carolina TV station, says that the change is long overdue and was delayed by economic considerations: "The real purpose in the quest for objectivity was the creation of a sterile environment to sell advertising" he says. In theory, controversy is not good for business; it frightens advertisers who don't want to alienate any potential customer. But Limbaugh's ratings—and the advertising revenues accompanying them—prove that audiences and theorists don't always think alike.

ON TO TELEVISION

"Rush Limbaugh: The Television Program."

It shouldn't work. It goes against all the rules of "good television." It should not be able to hold an audience.

Quoth Limbaugh, "Heh, heh, heh."

He makes it work. He is rewriting the rules. His audience is growing.

Limbaugh gives television viewers things they are not accustomed to. Instead of movement, electronic graphics, and other gimmicks, he sits at a desk and talks. Every so often he strolls to a nearby video monitor to introduce a brief videotaped piece. These sometimes feature a Clinton impersonator and often are TV news excerpts assembled (with surprising amateurishness) to tweak prominent liberals.

But most of the time he just sits behind his "Rush" nameplate, looks into the camera, and offers the day's wisdom. The talk is much like that on his radio show. But on TV, he relies exclusively on monologue, taking no calls and only occasionally engaging in some banter with a small but enthusiastic studio audience. His set resembles the dream den of a wealthy conservative—lots of dark wood and book shelves lined with many, many copies of the collected works (both volumes) of Rush Limbaugh.

He uses the camera well, flashing his winning smile, waggling a finger at the viewer to drive home his point. As much as he looks to be enjoying himself, Limbaugh also appears constrained by the thirty-minute format (about twenty-three minutes when commercials are subtracted). He rarely has time to heat up his rhetoric to full Limbaughesque boil, as he does in his three-hour radio show. And without callers he has no chance to display his skill as a verbal fencer.

Limbaugh clearly benefits from the guidance of his show's executive producer, Roger Ailes. Famous and infamous as media adviser to Ronald Reagan and George Bush, Ailes distilled his wisdom in his 1988 book, *You Are the Message: Secrets of the Master Communicators.* He offers concise tips, such as his "four essentials of a great communicator": Be prepared, make others comfortable, be committed, and be interesting. He explains how to manage energy, generate charisma, and tune in to an audience's mood.

Go down Ailes's list of what should be done and you'll find that Limbaugh excels in just about every category. Ever since he was a boy mimicking radio sportscasters, Limbaugh has been a good student, maybe not in school but certainly when focusing on matters in which he is interested. Under Ailes's tutelage, he has mastered the tools of his trade.

The show's audience growth reflects this. By summer 1993, Limbaugh's ratings had risen 38 percent since his program's debut in September 1992. In national ratings, Limbaugh ranked third behind ABC's "Nightline" and NBC's "Tonight Show," but finished well ahead of "Letterman" (the NBC version) and "Arsenio." The air times for Limbaugh vary from market to market because the show is syndicated, but in markets where he went head-to-head with his competition, Limbaugh narrowly bested "The Tonight Show," and had significantly higher ratings than "Letterman" and "Arsenio."[10]

As the second season for his show began in September 1993, Limbaugh reveled in the rising ratings and the improved time slots he was getting from the stations carrying him. At many stations, he had started out in the after-midnight schedule, targeted at college students, hip late-nighters, and insomniacs. But once he proved that people would watch as well as listen to a conservative polemicist, station managers became true believers. In some markets, he now appears in prime time.

"DE TALKVILLE"

Brought up in freedom that they usually take for granted, Americans are accustomed to talking whenever they want to. This seemed to de Tocqueville to be an important aspect of American democracy: "Men unacquainted with each other…find neither peril nor advantage in the free interchange of their thoughts." Their manner, he said, is "natural, frank, and open; it is easy to see that they hardly expect or apprehend anything from each other, and that they do not care to display, any more than to conceal, their position in the world." And, he added, if they do not talk at a particular time, "it is because they are not in a humor to talk, not because they think it in their interest to be silent."[11]

Although talk shows allow callers the shield of anonymity should they choose to use it, generally people do not fear reprisals or other negative repercussions if they participate in this forum. This means a huge reservoir of talkers exists, awaiting the stimulus of an interesting topic or provocative host.

This also means talk shows are likely to proliferate, especially on radio, where production costs are not as high as those for television. Using syndicated offerings usually cuts costs even further.

Virtually anywhere in America, you don't have to turn the radio dial very far before you come across a talk show. Sports programs give armchair quarterbacks opportunity to explain how their strategies would have won the game the day before. Medical show hosts will be happy to discuss your lower back pain. If you want to refinance your home, a financial talker will run the numbers for you. Want to sue someone? Try a legal call-in show. And when your car's brakes are squealing, there is "Car Talk," with brothers Tom and Ray Magliozzi (alias "Click and Clack") who, in their thick New England accents, will provide humorous and useful advice.

The list is likely to keep expanding. Even on television, new talk shows are popping up. For example, in Texas a clone of the Limbaugh show is being broadcast in the Dallas area. "Alex Burton Here" features long-time local radio commentator Alex Burton sitting at a desk with the daily newspaper spread open in front of him. He talks about whatever pops into his head. His politics are not as easy to discern as are Limbaugh's, and he lacks Limbaugh's compelling on-air presence. But the program provides a daily local fix for those talk show junkies who can't get enough of the genre.

All this public support for talk shows—and in some cases public reliance on them—fosters an electronic discourse that is part of the communications and information revolutions taking place as the twentieth century nears its end. This kind of conversation pushes aside other communicating. Why write to your elected official when you can broadcast your views on a call-in show? Why read your newspaper's opinion page when you can listen to Rush while you're driving your car?

Perhaps, despite Marshall McLuhan's dictum, the medium is not the entire message. But the medium shapes the message. And in the case of the talk show, the host shapes the medium.

LIMBAUGH FOREVER? 8

September 1993. The Clinton administration is unveiling its much-anticipated health-care reform program.

Tremendous effort goes into whipping up political support for the plan. The president and his surrogates fan out across the country. A rich diet of media events clogs the arteries of print and broadcast news organizations. Campaign '93 is rolling.

As a key element of this political plan, Clinton's strategists have invited talk show hosts to an exclusive White House briefing before the President addresses Congress and the nation. About seventy-five hosts plus producers and station executives show up and listen for three hours to the president plus Hillary Rodham Clinton,

Health and Human Services Secretary Donna Shalala, and others.

Mary Beal, president of the National Association of Talk Show Hosts, attends the White House meeting and notes the president's respect for talk shows' influence. "We are seen no longer as a stepchild," she says, "but as a validated medium ourselves. That is because we reach the people; we reach the grass roots. The president said, 'We (politicians) talk *to* the people, you talk *with* them.'"

The day after the speech to Congress, about sixty of the hosts are invited to do their shows live from the White House lawn. One reporter writes, "Set up on dozens of portable tables and chairs, the talk show hosts created a bizarre cacophony: a health-care gabfest that looked and sounded like Larry King meets Dr. Kildare."[1]

That night, Clinton travels to Tampa, Florida, to appear on a special prime-time edition of ABC's "Nightline." Sitting with Ted Koppel in the center of an auditorium filled with twelve hundred local residents, the president uses the town meeting/talk show format as effectively as he did during the previous year's campaign. Acting as empathetic listener and erudite teacher, Clinton is at his best. His performance is an essay in style—the style of a savvy politician and that of a successful talk show host. Increasingly, they are becoming one and the same.

BLAST THE BLITZ

Limbaugh had been invited to the White House briefing but declined, since it was scheduled for the same time as his radio program. The day after the Tampa show, he blasted away at the administration's public relations blitz.

Sounding like his always optimistic hero, Ronald Reagan, Limbaugh took umbrage at the administration's use of "crisis" to describe the state of American health care. He said, "I don't think we're in a crisis over anything."

He attacked the one-sidedness of the Clinton-orchestrated discussion of health care:

"When I say I am equal time, there's no better example."

To make his point, he devoted part of his show to calls from those supporting the Clinton plan. Strapping on his armor, mounting his charger, swinging his mace...Limbaugh was in his glory. He battled articulate callers and made his case against higher taxes and government intrusiveness with a mix of facts, opinion, and sarcasm. Some might challenge his treatment of such a complicated issue, but he said, "I like to make the complex things simple."

He had promised that both sides would be heard, and they were. But he always had the last word. As Limbaugh has said many times, his show exists to showcase his, not his callers', ideas.

UNFRIENDLY FIRE

The Clinton effort to use talk programs to their benefit reinforces the notion that this medium and its stars, such as Limbaugh, are extending their influence. For Limbaugh that promises to produce more fame, fortune, and power.

But it also means he will draw more fire from critics. For example, *Los Angeles Times* media writer Howard Rosenberg "decided to slide one of (Limbaugh's) TV half-hours under a microscope and study its molecular composition." He found a number of things to criticize:

- Host narcissism. The show contained forty-four references to Limbaugh in twenty-two minutes, and 32 percent of the show was devoted to Limbaugh and his ventures, such as his radio program.

- Using demeaning language. Limbaugh referred, for example, to a female Navy petty officer as a "sailorette." He added, "We say that with, of course, good cheer and no wish to offend."

- Using pejorative adjectives. For example, Limbaugh asked, "Have you noticed that militant environmentalists talk about the damage we're doing to the planet?" Rosenberg says that although Limbaugh's precise meaning of "militant" is unclear, it at the very least implies unsavory extremism.

Aside from Limbaugh's semantics, Rosenberg and other critics don't like what they say is an absence of fairness. Rosenberg wrote that Limbaugh's shows "are Maginot lines of conservatism that unfairly accommodate no opposing views." That is a particular problem on the television show since he takes no calls.

To counter such criticism, two points may be made:

- First, Limbaugh has no monopoly of the airwaves. Even if his opinion dominates his show, it is far from the only viewpoint that can be heard.

- Also, Limbaugh certainly features truth in packaging. No insidiously subtle mind-bending is going on. If you watch Limbaugh, you know you will get unadulterated conservatism.

Limbaugh also worries those who think he undermines government's credibility. These days, that isn't hard to do. Congressman Bill Hefner, a North Carolina Democrat and former radio broadcaster, says: "This thing scares me. There are so many cable channels and talk shows now, and they're nothing but negative attacks on institutions, especially government, at all levels. It's getting to the point where we're not able to govern."[2]

That might be an overstatement. Certainly, Limbaugh consistently condemns overreliance on government for welfare payments, health care, and other "entitlements." But he is no anarchist; he is not antigovernment per se, just anti-activist government. His position is no further from the mainstream than was President Reagan's, and his iconoclasm is milder than Ross Perot's.

To blame Limbaugh and like-minded talk show hosts for the decline in public faith in political institutions is buck-passing. Elected officials should look closer to home if they want to find the roots of dissatisfaction.

Some other anti-Limbaugh commentators leaven their criticism with bemusement and even grudging admiration for his style, if not his substance. Writing in *Commonweal*, Frank McConnell admitted to getting a kick out of Limbaugh because "he is basically the first truly postmodern conservative. His positions are, on the whole, deeply offensive to anybody who doesn't think that Pat Buchanan and Pat Robertson are, as I believe them to be, mutant aliens. But Rush, with sublime and often self-kidding humor, knows that the offensiveness is the gig....I'm not even sure, in fact that he mightn't be an agent provocateur, a crypto-liberal employed by, say, *Mother Jones* or the *Progressive* to make the ultraconservative stance so obviously untenable, such a parody of anything approaching responsible political speech, as to discredit it altogether as anything but entertainment."

Limbaugh never has shown himself to be greatly bothered by such criticism. After all, he has the ratings.

And he has gotten another nice reward for his ideological zeal—his very own presidential boomlet.

The Limbaugh-for-president tide ebbs and flows depending on the boredom and disenchantment levels of the moment. That the notion is discussed at all says something about the state of the Republican Party. Despite the army of wannabe presidents, no dominant figure has emerged as the principal anti-Clinton spokesman. Limbaugh, with his seventeen and a half hours of combined radio and TV time each week (not counting the repeats in many markets), is the nation's most visible Clinton basher.

That status leads to articles such as *National Review*'s "Leader of the Opposition" in September 1993, which poses the question, "What would make Rush run?" When asked about this, Limbaugh appears flattered but cautious. He is no fool. He understands, for instance, that even a listenership large enough to put him at the top of the ratings heap is far too small to win a national election.

In fact, Limbaugh's weekly audience of about twenty million is only about the size of Ross

Perot's 1992 vote, which was enough to earn Perot footnotes in history books, but translated into zero electoral votes. Limbaugh also can look at the unspectacular political careers of fellow broadcast talkers Pat Robertson and Pat Buchanan as object lessons about the perils of the hubris that media stardom fosters.

Limbaugh has said "never—ever" when asked if he will run, and cites having to "walk around with your hand out" asking for money as the main reason he doesn't want to do that. On the air, he is the master of his own fate. He has been doing his job and prospering. Why venture onto the politicians' turf and have to play by their rules?

Still, a Limbaugh candidacy is an intriguing enough idea to get some attention. Writing in the *Washington Post*, Richard Cohen made a good point: "For those tempted to scoff, I offer two words of warning: Ronald Reagan." Limbaugh's potential political strength, says Cohen, would be rooted in the same factors that fuel his popularity as a talk show host: voters' disillusionment with the mainstream media and their belief that their values are not reflected by the traditional wielders of power.

Limbaugh appears to be nowhere near galvanizing a true, Perot-like voter bloc. A July 1993 poll commissioned by *U.S. News and World Report* asked, "Should Limbaugh run for president?" The response: 8 percent yes, 57 percent no. Even among his most ardent listeners, only 17 percent said yes.

This is reflected in the calls that periodically come to Limbaugh's radio show, usually after a news story floats the presidential idea. Some callers say, "Rush we need you; go for it." Others, however, although clearly Limbaugh fans, are more cautious. They know, for one thing, that Limbaugh's accessibility would vanish if he became a candidate. He would lose his talk shows because of equal-time rules. He would have to make the compromises essential to getting elected. He would need to moderate his tone, his humor, and his philosophy to attract the mass of voters he would need to win. "Our Rush" would become "their Rush."

Limbaugh understands all that. He presumably would be happy to see William Bennett, Jack Kemp, or another conservative carry the GOP banner. He will probably content himself with looking at pictures of the White House, sighing resignedly, and then getting back to the business of liberal-bashing.

THE FAIRNESS DOCTRINE

Limbaugh's success has also pulled him into another controversy: the possible resurrection of the Fairness Doctrine.

Created by the Federal Communications Commission in 1949, the doctrine was based on the theory that disparate views needed guaranteed access to the limited number of radio and TV airwaves. As part of the deregulation trend during the Reagan years, the FCC abolished the rule in 1987. When Congress talked about enacting it into law, Reagan, and later George Bush, said they would veto it.

With Bill Clinton thought likely to sign such a bill, Fairness Doctrine proponents are reviving their efforts. The law would require broadcasters to provide time for alternative viewpoints to balance opinions being expressed on their air. That sounds reasonable enough, but in practice it would encourage stations to drop controversial programs.

This is why the bill is often referred to as the "anti-Limbaugh law," or, as Limbaugh himself calls it, the "hush Rush bill." The FCC's definition of "fairness" might require stations to maintain an equal number of liberal- and conservative-hosted programs, it might require issue-by-issue balancing, or it might necessitate parity in audience size.

For example, suppose a station carries Limbaugh and he is winning high ratings. To ensure "fairness," this station adds a show with a liberal host, but the ratings are far below Limbaugh's. If a regulation requiring balanced audience sizes was enacted, the station then would have to put Limbaugh on at 4:00 A.M. or some other atrocious time to drive his ratings down to match those of the opposition voice. That might sound ridiculous, but when the government gets into the business of defining and enforcing fairness, such farce could become commonplace.

Faced with this complexity, and with the threat of legal action and substantial fines hanging over their heads, many station executives would be tempted to drop Limbaugh and all other issues-related programming. Rock 'n' roll might be harder on the ears, but it could prove easier on the wallet.

Limbaugh knows he might be in jeopardy. "The Fairness Doctrine," he says, "is simply today's application of political correctness to the talk show business. Those with the real power are simply trying to stifle criticism, which, last time I looked, was protected speech."[3]

The argument against the doctrine is based partly on Constitutional principle and partly on the evolving technology of broadcast and cable communications. The average American home now receives thirty-five cable and broadcast channels, plus signals from at least dozens of radio stations.

On radio, for example, with more than eleven thousand stations broadcasting in the United

States, the open market can meet any reasonable demand for diverse opinions. Even absent much audience interest, so many electronic media vehicles are available that virtually any viewpoint can be heard. Community-access cable television is a good example. In the many communities where it is offered, even the smallest political faction has the opportunity to proselytize on TV.

Worth noting is the distinction legislators would make between print and electronic media. So far, the Supreme Court has allowed regulation of the airwaves and cable in ways that if applied to newspapers or magazines would certainly not withstand First Amendment challenge. This discrimination might have made sense when TV and radio broadcast channels were so few that regulating access to them seemed logical. But today, that is simply not the case.

In the fight against the Fairness Doctrine, Limbaugh has an unlikely ally—Mario Cuomo. The New York governor hosts his own monthly call-in show, making him more or less Limbaugh's professional colleague. In a *New York Times* op-ed column, Cuomo argued that reinstituting the doctrine would discourage public debate. He said the FCC knew of more than sixty reported instances of stations "quashing programming on such topics as the nuclear arms race, religious cults, and municipal salaries for fear of triggering fairness doctrine obligations."

Cuomo also addressed the ideological issue that generates impetus for a fairness law: "True progressives ought not be unnerved by the popularity of conservative talk show commentators. To safeguard our cherished freedom of expression, they should resist the temptation to stifle distasteful views and concentrate on sharpening their own."

Cuomo's argument makes sense. Liberals such as Cuomo or even Bill Clinton face no barriers to their using the airwaves as Limbaugh does. If you have something worth fighting for, get out and fight.

In a way, the push to bring back the Fairness Doctrine is a tribute to Limbaugh. Liberals are so aware that they have been outmaneuvered and outargued by him, that they try to re-engineer the playing field, using a federal statute as their steam-roller. The desire to strike out at Limbaugh is understandable in a political sense, but it certainly is a questionable basis for tampering with the First Amendment.

Limbaugh delights in calling himself "the poster boy of free speech." This struggle might end up with Limbaugh's constituency expanding to include those who see the Fairness Doctrine as an anti-free speech measure. Cuomo will probably be joined by some other liberals in opposing the legislation.

Rush Limbaugh and liberals on the same side! Look quickly; it won't last.

TECHNOLOGICAL REVOLUTION

National radio talk shows—such as Lim-baugh's—are creatures of relatively new satellite and tele-phone technology that have made affordable both access by callers and program acquisition by stations. The technological revolution is far from finished. As long as Limbaugh and his colleagues remain willing to adapt to change, they might find that their reach and influence will continue to grow.

One intriguing possibility now being developed is the use of the desktop personal computer as a talk radio medium. Using national and eventually global computer networks, a "radio talk show" can be "broadcast" to anyone who has the gear and desire to receive it. New computers have speakers, and sound can be digitized, so the show can be delivered as a digital computer file.

Digital transmission of video is likewise possible. Both radio- and TV-type networks will be accessible to millions once transmission lines and computer storage capabilities improve. They should reach the needed and affordable levels within the next few years.

Beyond the pure science of this is the considerable potential audience appeal. Among the capabilities of such a system are these:

- taking in the information and playing it whenever you desire (like videotaping a TV show for later viewing)

- altering the order of the programming

- participating in interactive programs, such as game shows in which everyone on-line can be a participant.

For a talk show host, the potential of this medium is tantalizing. The telephone would become unnecessary. The two-way information flow between host and listener would allow much more than the dialogue now heard on the air.

Suppose, for example, Limbaugh is touting capital gains tax reform. An interested listener could send a computer signal and have the details of Limbaugh's plan appear on the home computer screen, ready to be read and printed. The listener could then annotate Limbaugh's material and send it back. Forget fax machines.

Also, Limbaugh could urge that tidal waves of computer mail be unleashed on the White

House or elsewhere. Postcard and phone campaigns would be made obsolete by the ability to send faster and more detailed messages.

This carries electronic democracy to the next level. It is akin to the "electronic town meetings" Ross Perot touted in 1992. The two have similarities in their reach and also in their potential problems.

For instance, the representativeness of this computer jock audience might be questionable, especially during the early stages of this technology's use. Only those with the probably costly equipment could participate. So, the collective opinions they express—to Limbaugh or anyone else—should be recognized as coming from a narrow slice of the public and weighed accordingly.

Those who spend the money and time to plug into such programming are likely to be more politically active than is the average citizen. Such is the case with the C-SPAN audience. Although C-SPAN's programming reaches fifty-eight million homes, it usually has only two million viewers. But one survey found that 98 percent of this audience voted in 1992.[4]

The computer version of talk programming certainly will not put radio or TV out of business. It might cut into audience shares—more slicing of the pie—but mainly it is likely to expand overall audience. With more options for receiving the Limbaugh program and other talk shows, more people are likely to listen and talk. Given his adaptability and skill for self-promotion, Limbaugh surely will capitalize on any innovations.

LOOK OUT BELOW!

By late 1993, Limbaugh was on top of the world. The number of radio and television stations carrying his programs was growing and his ratings kept climbing. *The Way Things Ought to Be* passed its first anniversary on the hardcover best seller list and its softcover edition zoomed to the number one spot on the paperback list. His

second book, *See, I Told You So*, had a first print-
ing of more than a million copies and was another
immediate best seller. The monthly "Limbaugh
Letter" increased its subscriber list to nearly four
hundred thousand. Even magazines with his
picture on the cover sold out rapidly.

On the airwaves, Limbaugh became even
more ubiquitous, with brief updates being broadcast to tantalize listeners before the daily
three-hour program aired. Speculation continued
about a regular syndicated newspaper column and
maybe even a cartoon version of the Limbaugh
message. Who knows what will follow—Limbaugh
meets Disney?

Best of all for Limbaugh, he had Bill Clinton—
the personification of a liberalism that was oozing
out from behind a facade of centrism. Limbaugh
delighted in having a sparring mate whom he could
so freely pummel. For millions of conservatives,
Limbaugh was defender of the true faith, someone
they could turn to daily to be reassured by his
mellifluous preaching of their political gospel.

Limbaugh also had no shortage of reasons to blast Congress. One 1993 crusade was to pressure the House of Representatives to make public the names of members supporting discharge petitions used to bring bills from committee to the floor. This somewhat arcane issue was significant because it went to the heart of Congress's purported willingness to be more open, to let the American people see what the denizens of Capitol Hill actually do.

In this battle, Limbaugh was joined by members of Ross Perot's United We Stand America. For the moment, this was a one-shot alliance, but the prospect of Limbaugh-Perot cooperation must cause panic within the ranks of Washington insiders. (On other matters, such as the North American Free Trade Agreement, Limbaugh and Perot are on opposite sides.)

No clouds besides the Fairness Doctrine were to be seen on Limbaugh's horizon. Certainly, he was not menaced by competitors. Howard Stern was attracting large audiences with his trash talk, but his genre is different than Limbaugh's.

Ross Perot made his debut as a talk show host in September 1993 on CNBC, attracting callers voicing some of the same dissatisfaction Limbaugh so often hears. Perot has a folksy appeal. He told his first night's audience, "You can call in and we'll visit." But he is obviously advancing his personal agenda as presidential hopeful, and so lacks Limbaugh's credibility as selfless commentator about issues.

Talk show host association president Mary Beal, whose syndicated show is based in Wichita, Kansas, tries to put Limbaugh's success in perspective. "There are other talk show hosts around the country," she says, "just as talented and dynamic as Limbaugh is. He himself is not a phenomenon. He has a good product."

This product is Rush Limbaugh as a package. More than the conservative politics, more than the radio and TV shows, more than the newsletter and ninety-second updates, more than the books—the essence of Limbaugh's success is the collective mass of endeavors. The whole is greater than the sum of its parts.

The Limbaugh phenomenon is rooted in his personal drive and work ethic. He is on radio and TV air for a combined three and a half hours every weekday, plus generating all his other material, plus keeping up with the issues and events he wants to talk about. Not many people are willing to work that hard. Even his fiercest critics sometimes let a note of admiration slip into their comments about his work habits. His plaintiveness in interviews about his personal life offers some insight about how much he is paying for his success. But he is getting what he is paying for.

How long his preeminence will last is only partly a function of politics. Even if President Clinton accomplishes much of what he has set out to do and is hailed by his supporters as a latter-day FDR, substantial conservative opposition will remain. It might become even more virulent if

Clinton is successful. Limbaugh can count on finding a perpetual support base there.

The real key to Limbaugh's professional longevity will be his ability to maintain the self-discipline needed to make this one-man empire function.

Every indication is that he can do it.

And so, all you conversationalists across the fruited plain, worry not. With half his brain tied behind his back to make it a fair fight, the Godzilla of broadcasting will battle on.

Dittoheads rejoice; liberal wackos despair! Rush Limbaugh is likely to be with us for a long time.

NOTES

CHAPTER 1
1. James Bowman, "The Leader of the Opposition," *National Review* (September 6, 1993), 46.

2. Eric Morgenthaler, "A Common Touch," *The Wall Street Journal* (June 28, 1993), 1.

3. Joshua Hammer, "Welcome to Rush's World," *Newsweek* (September 28, 1992), 50.

CHAPTER 2
1. Maureen Dowd, "A Shy, Sensitive Guy Trying To Get By in Lib City," *The New York Times* (March 24, 1993), C 10.

2. Lewis Grossberger, "The Rush Hours," *The New York Times Magazine* (December 16, 1990), 95.

3. Paul D. Colford, *The Rush Limbaugh Story* (New York: St. Martin's, 1993), 26.

4. Steve Wulf (ed.), "Scorecard: Royal Rush," *Sports Illustrated* (March 1, 1993), 9.

5. Colford, *The Rush Limbaugh Story*, 52.

6. Grossberger, "The Rush Hours," 93.

7. Colford, *The Rush Limbaugh Story*, 123.

8. Rush Limbaugh, *The Way Things Ought to Be* (New York: Pocket Books, 1992), 21.

9. Dowd, "A Shy, Sensitive Guy," C 10.

10. Amy Bernstein, "Show Time in the Rush Room," *U.S. News and World Report* (August 16, 1993), 36.

11. Terry Eastland, "Rush Limbaugh: Talking Back," *The American Spectator* (September, 1992), 22.

12. Peter Viles, "For Limbaugh, Yet Another Ratings Rush," *Broadcasting and Cable* (March 8, 1993), 33.

13. Steven V. Roberts, "What a Rush!", *U.S. News and World Report* (August 16, 1993), 35.

14. Peter J. Boyer, "Bull Rush," *Vanity Fair* (May, 1992).

15. Ibid.

16. Roberts, "What a Rush!", 27.

17. Richard Corliss, "Conservative Provocateur or Big Blowhard," *Time* (October 26, 1992), 77.

18. Ibid.

19. Boyer, "Bull Rush."

20. Roberts, "What a Rush!", 30.

21. Corliss, "Conservative Provocateur," 77.

22. Colford, *The Rush Limbaugh Story*, 225.

23. Jack Germond and Jules Witcover, *Mad As Hell* (New York: Warner Books, 1993), 16.

24. Ibid., 510.

25. William J. Bennett, "Why Americans Are Angry: Rush Limbaugh on the Politics of 1992," *Policy Review* (Summer, 1992), 47.

26. Kiku Adatto, *Picture Perfect* (New York: Basic Books, 1993), 172.

27. Tom Rosenstiel, *Strange Bedfellows* (New York: Hyperion, 1993), 174.

28. Ibid., 182.

29. Bennett, "Why Americans Are Angry," 47.

30. Ibid.

31. Limbaugh, *The Way Things Ought to Be*, 289.

32. Colford, *The Rush Limbaugh Story*, 174.

33. Howard Kurtz, *Media Circus* (New York: Times Books, 1993), 364.

34. David S. Broder, *Behind the Front Page* (New York: Simon and Schuster, 1987), 12.

35. Rosenstiel, *Strange Bedfellows*, 154.

36. Twentieth Century Fund Task Force on Television and the Campaign of 1992, *1-800-President* (New York: The Twentieth Century Fund Press, 1993), 67.

37. Nelson W. Polsby and Aaron Wildavsky, *Presidential Elections* (sixth edition) (New York: Scribners, 1984), 72.

38. Roberts, "What a Rush!", 28.

39. Ibid., 35.

CHAPTER 3
1. Barry M. Goldwater with Jack Casserly, *Goldwater* (New York: Doubleday, 1988), 219.

2. Ibid., 390.

3. Theodore H. White, *The Making of the President 1964* (New York: Atheneum, 1965), 407.

4. Theodore H. White, *America in Search of Itself* (New York: Harper and Row, 1982), 241.

5. Limbaugh, *The Way Things Ought to Be*, 283.

6. James Q. Wilson, "Reagan and the Republican Revival," *Commentary* (October, 1980), 31.

7. Stephen E. Ambrose, *Nixon: The Education of a Politician 1913-1962* (New York: Simon and Schuster, 1987), 542.

8. Richard Reeves, *The Reagan Detour* (New York: Simon and Schuster, 1985), 10.

9. John Kenneth White, *The New Politics of Old Values* (Hanover, New Hampshire.: University Press of New England, 1988), 4.

10. Bennett, "Why Americans Are Angry," 48.

11. Garry Wills, *Reagan's America: Innocents at Home* (Garden City, New York: Doubleday, 1987), 4.

12. Ronnie Dugger, *On Reagan* (New York: McGraw-Hill, 1983), xiii.

13. J.K. White, *The New Politics of Old Values*, 143.

14. T.H. White, *America in Search of Itself*, 306.

15. Jonathan Schell, *History in Sherman Park* (New York: Knopf, 1987), 5.

16. William A. Henry III, *Visions of America* (Boston: Atlantic Monthly Press, 1985), 263.

17. George F. Will, *Suddenly* (New York: The Free Press, 1992), 160.

18. Ibid., 283.

19. Michael Duffy and Dan Goodgame, *Marching in Place* (New York: Simon and Schuster, 1992), 22.

20. Margaret Carlson, "An Interview with Rush Limbaugh," *Time* (October 26, 1992), 79.

21. Germond and Witcover, *Mad As Hell*, 23.

CHAPTER 4
1. Germond and Witcover, Mad *As Hell*, 35.

2. Rosentstiel, *Strange Bedfellows*, 137.

3. J.K. White, *The New Politics of Old Values*, 74.

4. Peter Brown, *Minority Party* (Washington: Regnery Gateway, 1991), ix.

5. Ibid., 316.

6. Douglas Harbrecht, "A Fleeting Victory for Conservative Democrats?", *Business Week* (May 11, 1992), 49.

7. Brown, *Minority Party*, 321.

8. Limbaugh, *The Way Things Ought to Be*, 225.

9. Michael Kelly, "President's Early Troubles Rooted in Party's Old Strains," *The New York Times* (February 2, 1993), A 1.

10. Wayne Walley, "Election's End Won't Be the Last of Limbaugh," *Electronic Media* (November 16, 1992).

11. John Kenneth Galbraith, *The Culture of Contentment* (New York: Houghton Mifflin, 1992), 14.

CHAPTER 5

1. Rosenstiel, *Strange Bedfellows*, 168.

2. Henry David Thoreau, *Walden* (New York: Bramhall House, 1951), 67.

3. Marilyn J. Matelski, "Resilient Radio," *Media Studies Journal* (Summer, 1993), 1.

4. Arthur Frank Wertheim, *Radio Comedy* (New York: Oxford University Press, 1979), 6.

5. Roberts, "What a Rush!", 35.

6. John Dunning, *Tune in Yesterday* (Englewood Cliffs, New Jersey: Prentice-Hall, 1976), 45.

7. Reed E. Bunzel, "Garrison Keillor: An American Radio Romance," *Broadcasting* (January 6, 1992), 86.

8. Ibid., 84.

9. Edward R. Murrow, *The Broadcasts of Edward R. Murrow* (New York: Knopf, 1967), 35.

10. A.M. Sperber, *Murrow: His Life and Times* (New York: Freundlich Books, 1986), 110.

11. Joseph E. Persico, *Edward R. Murrow: An American Original* (New York: McGraw-Hill, 1988), 245.

12. Ibid., 103.

13. David Bartlett, "News Radio—More Than Masters of Disaster," *Media Studies Journal* (Summer, 1993), 39.

14. Ibid., 49.

15. Edward W. Chester, *Radio, Television and American Politics* (New York: Sheen and Ward, 1969), 194.

16. Alan Brinkley, *Voices of Protest* (New York: Knopf, 1982), 97.

17. James MacGregor Burns, *Roosevelt: The Lion and the Fox* (New York: Harcourt, Brace and World, 1956), 212.

18. Chester, *Radio, Television and American Politics*, 196.

19. Brinkley, *Voices of Protest*, 96.

20. William Ivy Hair, *The Kingfish and His Realm* (Baton Rouge, Louisiana: Louisiana State University Press, 1991), 285.

21. James A. Farley, *Behind the Ballots* (New York: Harcourt, Brace, 1938), 249.

22. Bowman, "The Leader of the Opposition," 46.

23. Arthur Frank Wertheim, *Radio Comedy* (New York: Oxford University Press, 1979), 63.

24. Michael X. Delli Carpini, "Radio's Political Past," *Media Studies Journal* (Summer, 1993), 28.

25. Ibid., 32.

26. Wills, *Reagan's America*, 99.

27. Ronald Reagan, *An American Life* (New York: Simon and Schuster, 1990), 247.

28. Lou Cannon, *Reagan* (New York: Putnam, 1982), 196.

CHAPTER 6
1. Reed E. Bunzel, "Talk Networks Pursue Role of AM 'White Knight'," *Broadcasting* (August 27, 1990), 40.

2. Peter Fornatale and Joshua Mills, *Radio in the Television Age* (Woodstock, New York: The Overlook Press, 1980), 85.

3. Peter Viles, "Talk Radio a Player in Presidential Campaign," *Broadcasting* (June 15, 1992), 14.

4. Catherine Field, "Talk on Radio Show Was Too Frank for China's Old Guard," *The Dallas Morning News* (September 2, 1993).

5. Bruce Watson, "The Topic for Today: How Much More Talk Radio Can You Take?", *Smithsonian* (July, 1993), 20.

6. Peter Viles, "AM Radio's One-Man Comeback," *Broadcasting* (May 4, 1992), 55.

7. James C. Roberts, "The Power of Talk Radio," *The American Enterprise* (May-June, 1991), 59.

8. Times Mirror Center for The People and The Press, *The Vocal Minority in American Politics* (July, 1993).

9. Limbaugh, *The Way Things Ought to Be*, 269.

10. Dirk Smillie, "Talking to America: The Rise of Talk Shows in the '92 Campaign," *The Media and Campaign '92: An Uncertain Season* (New York: The Freedom Forum Media Studies Center, 1992), 26.

11. Viles, "Talk Radio a Player," 14.

12. Carolyn Barta, *Perot and His People* (Fort Worth, Texas: The Summit Group, 1993), 396.

13. Ibid., 393.

14. Rosenstiel, *Strange Bedfellows*, 175.

15. Germond and Witcover, *Mad As Hell*, 288.

16. Rosenstiel, *Strange Bedfellows*, 316.

17. Ibid., 164.

18. Ibid., 165.

19. Ibid., 167.

20. Limbaugh, *The Way Things Ought to Be*, 3.

21. Barta, *Perot and His People*, 390.

22. Peter Viles, "Hosts, Callers Trash Clinton on Talk Radio," *Broadcasting and Cable* (July 12, 1993), 42.

23. S. Roberts, "What a Rush!", 30.

24. Elizabeth Kolbert, "My Next Guest's Policy Opens Today!", *The New York Times* (September 10, 1993), A 12.

CHAPTER 7
1. Limbaugh, *The Way Things Ought to Be*, 21.

2. Colford, *The Rush Limbaugh Story*, 221.

3. Rosenstiel, *Strange Bedfellows*, 170.

4. Germond and Witcover, *Mad As Hell*, 276.

5. Rosenstiel, *Strange Bedfellows,* 168.

6. Bill Turque, "Press '1' for the Christian Right," *Newsweek* (February 8, 1993), 28.

7. Neil Postman, *Amusing Ourselves to Death* (New York: Viking, 1985), 117.

8. Alan Hirsch, *Talking Heads* (New York: St. Martin's, 1991), 47.

9. David Shenk, "A Case of Kinsleyitis," *The Washington Post* (August 8, 1993), C 1.

10. Mike Freeman, "Whitney, Limbaugh Make Late-Night Moves," *Broadcasting and Cable* (August 23, 1993), 28.

11. Alexis de Tocqueville, *Democracy in America* (New York: Mentor/New American Library, 1956), 222.

CHAPTER 8
1. Thomas L. Friedman, "Clinton's Campaign '93: A Road Tour With Answers for All," *The New York Times* (September 24, 1993), A 12.

2. S. Roberts, "What a Rush!", 30.

3. Jim Cooper, "Talkers Brace for 'Fairness' Assault," *Broadcasting and Cable* (September 6, 1993), 44.

4. Howard Fineman, "The Power of Talk," *Newsweek* (February 8, 1993), 26.

BIBLIOGRAPHY

Adatto, Kiku. *Picture Perfect*. New York: Basic Books, 1993.

Ailes, Roger with Kraushar, Jon. *You Are the Message*. Homewood, Illinois: Dow Jones-Irwin, 1988.

Ambrose, Stephen E. *Nixon: The Education of a Politician 1913-1962*. New York: Simon and Schuster, 1987.

Arkush, Michael. *Rush!* New York: Avon, 1993.

Barta, Carolyn. *Perot and His People*. Fort Worth, Texas: The Summit Group, 1993.

Bartlett, David. "News Radio—More Than Masters of Disaster." *Media Studies Journal*, Summer, 1993.

Bennett, William J. "Why Americans Are Angry: Rush Limbaugh on the Politics of 1992." *Policy Review*, Summer, 1992, Number 61.

Berke, Richard L. "Poll Says Conservatives Dominate Talk Radio." *The New York Times*, July 16, 1993.

Bernstein, Amy. "Show Time in the Rush Room." *U.S. News and World Report*, August 16, 1993.

Bowman, James. "The Leader of the Opposition." *National Review*, September 6, 1993.

Boyer, Peter J. "Bull Rush." *Vanity Fair*, May, 1992.

Brinkley, Alan. *Voices of Protest*. New York: Knopf, 1982.

Broder, David S. *Behind the Front Page*. New York: Simon and Schuster, 1987.

Brown, Peter. *Minority Party*. Washington: Regnery Gateway, 1991.

Bunzel, Reed E. "Garrison Keillor: An American Radio Romance." *Broadcasting*, January 6, 1992.

——. "Talk Networks Pursue Role of AM 'White Knight'." *Broadcasting*, August 27, 1990.

Burns, James MacGregor. *Roosevelt: The Lion and the Fox*. New York: Harcourt, Brace and World, 1956.

Bush, George with Gold, Victor. *Looking Forward*. New York: Bantam, 1988.

Cannon, Lou. *Reagan*. New York: Putnam, 1982.

Carbaugh, Donal. *Talking American*. Norwood, New Jersey: Ablex Publishing, 1988.

Carlson, Margaret. "An Interview with Rush Limbaugh." *Time*, October 26, 1992.

Castro, Janice. "Grapevine: Left Out." *Time*, February 8, 1993.

——. "Grapevine: The Limbaugh State." *Time*, October 19, 1992.

Chester, Edward W. *Radio, Television and American Politics*. New York: Sheen and Ward, 1969.

Cohen, Richard. "President Limbaugh?" *The Washington Post*, September 7, 1993.

Colford, Paul D. *The Rush Limbaugh Story*. New York: St. Martin's, 1993.

Cooper, Jim. "Talkers Brace for 'Fairness' Assault." *Broadcasting and Cable*, September 6, 1993.

Corliss, Richard. "Conservative Provocateur or Big Blowhard." *Time*, October 26, 1992.

Cuomo, Mario. "The Unfairness Doctrine." *The New York Times*, September 20, 1993.

Deaver, Michael K. with Mickey Herskowitz. *Behind the Scenes*. New York: William Morrow, 1987.

Delli Carpini, Michael X. "Radio's Political Past." *Media Studies Journal*, Summer, 1993.

Diamond, Edwin. "Roger and Me." *New York*, September 28, 1992.

Dionne, E.J., Jr. *Why Americans Hate Politics*. New York: Touchstone/Simon and Schuster, 1992.

Dowd, Maureen. "A Shy, Sensitive Guy Trying to Get By in Lib City." *The New York Times*, March 24, 1993.

Duffy, Michael and Goodgame, Dan. *Marching in Place*. New York: Simon and Schuster, 1992.

Dugger, Ronnie. *On Reagan*. New York: McGraw-Hill, 1983.

Dunning, John. *Tune In Yesterday*. Englewood Cliffs, New Jersey: Prentice-Hall, 1976.

Eastland, Terry. "Rush Limbaugh: Talking Back." *The American Spectator*, September, 1992.

Farley, James A. *Behind the Ballots*. New York: Harcourt, Brace, 1938.

Field, Catherine. "Talk on Radio Show Was Too Frank for China's Old Guard." *The Dallas Morning News*, September 2, 1993.

Fineman, Howard. "The Power of Talk." *Newsweek*, February 8, 1993.

Fornatale, Peter and Joshua Mills. *Radio in the Television Age*. Woodstock, New York: The Overlook Press, 1980.

Freeman, Mike. "Whitney, Limbaugh Make Late-Night Moves." *Broadcasting and Cable*, August 23, 1993.

Friedman, Thomas L. "Clinton's Campaign '93: A Road Tour With Answers for All." *The New York Times*, September 24, 1993.

Galbraith, John Kenneth. *The Culture of Contentment*. New York: Houghton Mifflin, 1992.

Germond, Jack and Jules Witcover. *Mad As Hell*. New York: Warner Books, 1993.

Goldwater, Barry M. with Casserly, Jack. *Goldwater*. New York: Doubleday, 1988.

Goodman, Walter. "He's No. 1." *The New York Times Book Review*, February 21, 1993.

Grossberger, Lewis. "The Rush Hours." *The New York Times Magazine*, December 16, 1990.

Hair, William Ivy. *The Kingfish and His Realm*. Baton Rouge, Louisiana: Louisiana State University Press, 1991.

Hammer, Joshua. "Welcome to Rush's World." *Newsweek*, September 28, 1992.

Harbrecht, Douglas. "A Fleeting Victory for Conservative Democrats?" *Business Week*, May 11, 1992.

Heaton, Terry. "A News Director's View: Limbaugh Breath of Fresh Air." *Electronic Media*, November 16, 1992.

Henry, William A. III. *Visions of America*. Boston: Atlantic Monthly Press, 1985.

Hess, Karl. *In a Cause That Will Triumph*. New York: Doubleday, 1967.

Hirsch, Alan. *Talking Heads*. New York: St. Martin's, 1991.

Johnson, Haynes. *Sleepwalking Through History*. New York: W.W. Norton, 1991.

Judis, John B. "The Old Democrat." *The New Republic*, February 22, 1993.

Kelly, Michael. "'New Democrats' Say Clinton Has Veered Left and Left Them." *The New York Times*, May 23, 1993.

——. "President's Early Troubles Rooted in Party's Old Strains." *The New York Times*, February 2, 1993.

Kemp, Jack. *An American Renaissance*. New York: Harper and Row, 1979.

Ketchum, Richard M. *Will Rogers: The Man and His Times*. New York: American Heritage, 1973.

Kolbert, Elizabeth. "My Next Guest's Policy Opens Today!" *The New York Times*, September 10, 1993.

——. "The People Are Heard, at Least Those Who Call Talk Radio." *The New York Times*, January 29, 1993.

Kosof, Anna. "Public Radio—Americans Want More." *Media Studies Journal*, Summer, 1993.

Kurtz, Howard. *Media Circus*. New York: Times Books, 1993.

Lee, Judith Yaross. *Garrison Keillor: A Voice of America*. Jackson, Mississippi: University Press of Mississippi, 1991.

Levin, Murray B. *Talk Radio and the American Dream*. Lexington, Massachusetts: D.C. Heath/ Lexington Books, 1987.

Lewis, Tom. "Triumph of the Idol—Rush Limbaugh and a Hot Medium." *Media Studies Journal*, Summer, 1993.

"Lexington." "Talk-Radio Meets Rock-TV." *The Economist*, September 5, 1992.

Limbaugh, Rush. "Get Angry, Bush." *The New York Times*, October 15, 1992.

——. "Turn the Voters Loose." *National Review*, October 5, 1992.

———. *The Way Things Ought to Be*. New York: Pocket Books, 1992.

Markoff, John. "Turning the Desktop PC Into a Talk Radio Medium." *The New York Times*, March 4, 1993.

Matelski, Marilyn J. "Resilient Radio." *Media Studies Journal*, Summer, 1993.

McConnell, Frank. "It's Not Hell, Just Limbaugh." *Commonweal*, June 4, 1993.

Morgenthaler, Eric. "A Common Touch." *The Wall Street Journal*, June 28, 1993.

Murrow, Edward R. *The Broadcasts of Edward R. Murrow*. New York: Knopf, 1967.

Persico, Joseph E. *Edward R. Murrow: An American Original*. New York: McGraw-Hill, 1988.

Polsby, Nelson W. and Wildavsky, Aaron. *Presidential Elections* (sixth edition). New York: Scribners, 1984.

Postman, Neil. *Amusing Ourselves to Death*. New York: Viking, 1985.

Powell, Adam Clayton III. "You Are What You Hear." *Media Studies Journal*, Summer, 1993.

Raspberry, William. "Rushing from Judgment." *Dallas Morning News*, March 3, 1993.

Reagan, Ronald. *An American Life*. New York: Simon and Schuster, 1990.

Reeves, Richard. *The Reagan Detour*. New York: Simon and Schuster, 1985.

Rehm, Diane. "Talking Over America's Electronic Backyard Fence." *Media Studies Journal*, Summer, 1993.

Roberts, James C. "The Power of Talk Radio." *The American Enterprise*, May-June, 1991.

Roberts, Steven V. "What a Rush!" *U.S. News and World Report*, August 16, 1993.

Rosenstiel, Tom. *Strange Bedfellows*. New York: Hyperion, 1993.

Rusher, William A. *The Rise of the Right*. New York: William Morrow, 1984.

Schell, Jonathan. *History in Sherman Park*. New York: Knopf, 1987.

Seib, Philip. *Campaigns and Conscience: The Ethics of Political Journalism*. New York: Praeger, 1994.

Shaw, David. "Media Credibility Sinking." *The Dallas Morning News*, June 20, 1993.

Shenk, David. "A Case of Kinsleyitis." *The Washington Post*, August 8, 1993.

Smillie, Dirk. "Talking to America: The Rise of Talk Shows in the '92 Campaign." *The Media and Campaign '92: An Uncertain Season*. New York: The Freedom Forum Media Studies Center, 1992.

Sperber, A.M. *Murrow: His Life and Times*. New York: Freundlich Books, 1986.

Sterling, Christopher and John M. Kitross. *Stay Tuned*. Belmont, California: Wadsworth, 1978.

Stern, Kenneth. *Hate on Talk Radio*. New York: The American Jewish Committee, 1991.

Stockman, David A. *The Triumph of Politics*. New York: Harper and Row, 1986.

Thomas, Cal. "Rebirth of Fairness Doctrine." *The Dallas Morning News*, September 2, 1993.

Thoreau, Henry David. *Walden*. New York: Bramhall House, 1951.

Times Mirror Center for The People and The Press. "The Press and Campaign '92: A Self-Assessment." *Columbia Journalism Review*, March/April, 1993.

——. *The Vocal Minority in American Politics*. July, 1993.

Tocqueville, Alexis de. *Democracy in America*. New York: Mentor/New American Library, 1956.

Turque, Bill. "Press '1' for the Christian Right." *Newsweek*, February 8, 1993.

Twentieth Century Fund Task Force on Television and the Campaign of 1992, *1-800-President*. New York: The Twentieth Century Fund Press, 1993.

Viles, Peter. "AM Radio's One-Man Comeback." *Broadcasting*, May 4, 1992.

——. "Coming Soon: Talk Radio Via PC." *Broadcasting and Cable*, March 22, 1993.

——. "For Limbaugh, Yet AnOther Ratings Rush." *Broadcasting and Cable*, March 8, 1993, p. 33.

——. "Hosts, Callers Trash Clinton on Talk Radio." *Broadcasting and Cable*, July 12, 1993, p. 42.

——. "Radio Syndication." *Broadcasting and Cable*, May 17, 1993.

——. "Talk Radio a Player in Presidential Campaign." *Broadcasting*, June 15, 1992.

——. "Talk Radio Riding High." *Broadcasting*, June 15, 1992.

"Vox Populi." *The Nation*, March 1, 1993.

Walley, Wayne. "Election's End Won't Be Last of Limbaugh." *Electronic Media*, November 16, 1992.

Watson, Bruce. "The Topic for Today: How Much More Talk Radio Can You Take?" *Smithsonian*, July, 1993.

Wertheim, Arthur Frank. *Radio Comedy*. New York: Oxford University Press, 1979.

Whetmore, Edward Jay. *The Magic Medium*. Belmont, California: Wadsworth, 1981.

White, John Kenneth. *The New Politics of Old Values*. Hanover, New Hampshire: University Press of New England, 1988.

White, Theodore H. *America in Search of Itself*. New York: Harper and Row, 1982.

———. *The Making of the President 1964*. New York: Atheneum, 1965.

Will, George F. *Suddenly*. New York: The Free Press, 1992.

Wills, Garry. *Reagan's America: Innocents at Home*. Garden City, New York: Doubleday, 1987.

Wilson, James Q. "Reagan and the Republican Revival." *Commentary*, October, 1980.

Wolcott, James. "Rush Judgment." *The New Yorker*, February 22, 1993.

Wulf, Steve (ed.) "Scorecard: Royal Rush." *Sports Illustrated*, March 1, 1993.

INDEX